In celebration of 25 years of Educational and Child Psychology

EDUCATIONAL AND CHILD PSYCHOLOGY
VOLUME 25, NUMBER 4

Guest editors

Phil Stringer & Andy Miller

Contents

Contents

About the contributors

Theresa Bolton is an Educational Psychologist with East Sussex Educational Psychology Service.

Joe Dawson is Acting Principal Educational Psychologist with Leicester City Educational Psychology Service.

Andrea Dennison is an Educational Psychologist with Dorset Educational Psychology Service.

Christine Devonshire is an Educational Psychologist with Leicester City Educational Psychology Service.

Sue Fairhurst is a Senior Educational Psychologist (Early Years) with South Gloucestershire Educational Psychology Service.

Alison Farmer is an Acting Principal Educational Psychologist with Camden Educational Psychology Service.

Peter Farrell is Sarah Fielden Professor of Special Needs and Educational Psychology in the School of Education, University of Manchester.

John Franey is Programme Director for the Doctoral Training Programme in Educational Psychology at the University of Bristol.

Alison Gardener is a Specialist Senior Educational Psychologist with Northamptonshire Educational Psychology Service.

Simon Gibbs is a Senior Lecturer in Educational Psychology and Course Director for the DAppEdPsy, School of Education, Communication and Language Sciences, Newcastle University.

Charlie Gow is an Educational Psychologist with the North Lanarkshire Psychological Service.

Carole Jones is an Educational Psychologist with Derby City Educational Psychology Service.

Miriam Landor is an Educational Psychologist with West Lothian Psychological Service.

Sheila Leech is an Educational Psychologist with South Gloucestershire Educational Psychology Service.

Tom Lowe is a Senior Educational Psychologist with the North Lanarkshire Psychological Service.

Anne Matthews is a Senior Educational Psychologist with Leicestershire Educational Psychology Service.

Caoimhe Mcbay is an Educational Psychologist with Islington Educational Psychology Service.

Deborah Middleton is an Educational Psychologist with South Gloucestershire Educational Psychology Service.

Contributors

Andy Miller is a Special Professor of Educational Psychology at the University of Nottingham School of Psychology.

Heather Northcote is an Educational Psychologist with Derbyshire Educational Psychology Service.

Anne Powell-Davies is a Senior Educational Psychologist & Telford Team Leader with Shropshire, Telford and Wrekin Educational Psychology Service.

Philip Prior is Principal Educational Psychologist with Wandsworth Educational Psychology Service.

Chris Shaldon is an Educational Psychologist with Islington Educational Psychology Service.

Kathie Souter is a Freelance Educational Psychologist based in Bath.

Phil Stringer is County Services Manager (Educational Psychology Service, Behaviour Support Service, School Counselling Service) with Hampshire County Council Children's Services Department.

Laura Walmsley is an Educational Psychologist with North Lanarkshire Psychological Service.

Hugh Watson is an Educational Psychologist with Cambridgeshire Educational Psychology Service.

Peter Wiggs is Principal Educational Psychologist with South Gloucestershire Educational Psychology Service.

General Editorial

Twenty-five years of Educational and Child Psychology

Simon Gibbs

I T IS a great privilege to be the incumbent general editor of *Educational and Child Psychology* as it reaches its silver jubilee. As Phil Stringer and Andy Miller observe in their editorial, successive parts, since its inception in 1985, have provided a showcase of writing talent from a range of practitioners and related academic researchers. The particularly distinctive feature of having many of the early volumes, and all of the later ones, organised around a professionally pertinent and contemporary theme has served the publication well. The papers selected for republication here, and the accompanying accounts from the various colleagues on the judging panels, attest to the breadth, liveliness and, most significantly, professional relevance of the publication's content.

But another significant feature of *Educational and Child Psychology*, and one that makes a further contribution to its overall impact, is the long established tradition of guest editors taking responsibility for the production of issues. Promoting participation in the publication in this way has become an important principle.

For some while now, the editorial board has been responsible for identifying current topics that may form the basis of future issues, although occasionally someone outside the editorial board approaches me with a suggestion. As the production schedule for any part of a volume, from the identification of a topic through to the final publication arriving with subscribers, occupies a time span of at least 12 to 18 months, this aspect of the work of the editorial board has to not only reflect topicality, it has if at all possible to also employ a decent measure of prescience as well.

If one or more guest editors haven't offered their services through suggesting a topic, the editorial board generates a list of possible guest editors and approaches to the selected colleagues are then made. Once these guest editors have agreed to take on the task, with assistance from a member of the Board, a call for papers is issued through a number of routes. The usual processes of anonymous 'blind' refereeing by members of the editorial board and other seconded experts in the topic area then takes place and after any required revisions and further proof editing, the final selected papers are passed to the general editor to work with the Society on typesetting and distribution.

Readers will see from the accompanying table that the publication has been fortunate in the extreme in the list of prestigious guest editors who have taken on the not inconsiderable task of producing a themed issue. Indeed, many have returned more than once. The list itself reads like a roll call of the many leading thinkers and practitioners from the profession of educational psychology, with training course directors and tutors and principal educational psychologists featuring heavily among their numbers. Some have moved on to other career options, some have retired, and among their number we can count no fewer than 15 university professors. The major commitment made by these colleagues to maintaining and extending the flow of high quality publications, some of them ground-breaking in their time, and navigating all the unseen stresses and deadlines that are the lot of any editor, is to be applauded.

The profession is fortunate indeed to have, and to have had, such colleagues step forward to take up this challenge. This publication owes a huge debt of gratitude to all its many contributors, authors and editors alike. Phil and Andy stand in line with that tradition and I am enormously grateful to them for compiling this issue. Perhaps only those who have taken on a task of this nature can appreciate what it involves: time, care and energy especially. This particular edition has, I am sure, taken Phil and Andy down many a 'memory lane'. We are fortunate to have such colleagues who can take such a careful overview of this publication and, in many senses, of the profession of educational psychology. I trust that you will agree that this special jubilee edition provides a showcase and a fascinating historical glimpse into the variety and quality of papers contained within the publication over the past 25 years.

Simon Gibbs

Address for correspondence

Dr Simon Gibbs, Senior Lecturer in Educational Psychology and Course Director for the DAppEdPsy, School of Education, Communication and Language Sciences, Newcastle University, King George VI Building, Newcastle upon Tyne, NE1 7RU. E-mail: s.j.gibbs@newcastle.ac.uk

---

Citation Warning
Many of the reprinted articles were published at a time when there were different citation standards. There has been no attempt to update articles in this respect and, accordingly, we apologise to any reader who is left puzzling about the source of a reference.

Celebrating 25 volumes of Editors

The volume number and year of publication is followed by issue number and the name(s) of the editor(s) for that issue. The first three volumes and volume seven only comprised three issues.

Volume 1	1984	No 1 No 2 No 3	Peter Pumfrey Sean Cameron Sean Cameron
Volume 2	1985	No 1 No 2 No 3	Bob Burden Bob Stratford Geoff Lindsay
Volume 3	1986	No 1 No 2 No 3	Richard Williams, Peter Portwood Richard Williams, Peter Portwood Ingrid Lunt, John Shepherd
Volume 4	1987	No 1 No 2 No 3 No 4	John Thacker, Richard Williams John Thacker, Richard Williams John Thacker, Richard Williams John Thacker, Richard Williams
Volume 5	1988	No 1 No 2 No 3 No 4	Rea Reason, Richard Williams Sheila Wolfendale, Ingrid Lunt, Tim Carroll Bob Burden Bob Burden
Volume 6	1989	No 1 No 2 No 3 No 4	Geoff Lindsay, Anne Peake Frank Besag Terri-Anne Hornby, Vanessa Parffrey Terri-Anne Hornby, Vanessa Parffrey
Volume 7	1990	No 1 No 2 No 3	Rea Reason, Richard Williams Malcolm Gledhill, Rea Reason Peter Gray, Ingrid Lunt
Volume 8	1991	No 1 No 2 No 3 No 4	Peter Gray, Geoff Lindsay Ingrid Lunt, John Shepherd Alec Webster Ingrid Lunt
Volume 9	1992	No 1 No 2 No 3 No 4	Philip Jones, Theresa Crowley-Bainton Peter Gray Anne Peake Stephanie Lorenz, Peter Gray
Volume 10	1993	No 1 No 2 No 3 No4	Frank Besag, Richard Wiliams Ingrid Lunt, Mike Pomerantz Liz Malcolm, Anne Peake, Sonia Sharp, Chris Walker Julian Elliot, Joan Figg
Volume 11	1994	No 1 No 2 No 3 No 4	Joan Figg Bob Burden Derek Indoe, Chris Spencer Mary John
Volume 12	1995	No 1 No 2 No 3 No 4	Norah Frederickson, Rea Reason Derek Indoe, Ingrid Lunt, Rob Stoker Jenny Parkes, Sonia Sharp, Chris Spencer, Ros Vahey Derek Indoe, Andrea Pecherek

Voume 13	1996	No 1 No 2 No 3 No 4	Derek Indoe, Ingrid Lunt, Sheila Wolfendale Simon Gibbs, Rob Stoker Ingrid Lunt, Sonia Sharp, Rob Stoker Rob Stoker, Chris Walker
Volume 14	1997	No 1 No 2 No 3 No 4	Rea Reason, Sonia Sharp Anne Peake Chris Walker Julian Elliott, Fraser Lauchlan, Phil Stringer
Volume 15	1998	No 1 No 2 No 3 No 4	Patti Harrison, Derek Indoe Rob Stoker Ingrid Lunt Simon Gibbs
Volume 16	1999	No 1 No 2 No 3 No 4	James Boyle, Tommy MacKay Joan Figg Shunga M'gadzah, Simon Gibbs Simon Gibbs
Volume 17	2000	No 1 No 2 No 3 No 4	Peter Lloyd Bennett Joan Figg, Simon Gibbs Jullian Elliott Simon Gibbs
Volume 18	2001	No 1 No 2 No 3 No 4	Jeremy Monsen Peter Lloyd Bennett, Tom Billington Julian Elliott, Simon Gibbs Simon Gibbs
Volume 19	2002	No 1 No 2 No 3 No 4	Alec Webster, Peter Lloyd Bennett Carol Aubrey, Joan Figg Andy Miller, Simon Gibbs Simon Gibbs
Volume 20	2003	No 1 No2 No 3 No 4	Tom Billington, Sam Warner Joan Figg, Julian Elliott Susan Pickering Simon Gibbs
Volume 21	2004	No 1 No 2 No 3 No 4	Geerdina Maria van der Aalsvoort, Guenther Opp Peter Lloyd Bennett Phil Stringer, David Bracher Simon Gibbs
Volume 22	2005	No 1 No 2 No 3 No 4	Jane Leadbetter, Harry Daniels, Phil Stringer Nadina Lincoln, Simon Gibbs Peter Lloyd Bennett, Diny van der Aalsvoort Simon Gibbs
Volume 23	2006	No 1 No 2 No 3 No 4	Phil Stringer, Peter Jones Neil Ryrie, Claire Lawrence, Andy Miller Wilma Resing, Joan Figg Andy Miller, Anthea Gulliford, Phil Stringer
Volume 24	2007	No 1 No 2 No 3 No 4	Tommy MacKay, Anne Greig Penelope Munn, Rea Reason Diny van der Aalsvoort, Julian Elliott Nicola Botting, Wilma Resing
Volume 25	2008	No 1 No 2 No 3 No 4	Simon Gibbs Sue Roffey, Toni Noble, Phil Stringer Simon Gibbs, Diny van der Aalsvoort, Claudine Crane Phil Stringer, Andy Miller

Editorial

In celebration of the educational psychologist as a scientist practitioner

Phil Stringer & Andy Miller

WRITING ABOUT the theory and practice of educational psychologists has been a feature of the profession ever since its inception. Despite the later controversy that came to surround the first educational psychologist (EP) in the UK, Sir Cyril Burt, no one suggests that he fabricated every one of the 20 books and 300 articles or so that he wrote. Burt was an archetypical scientist–practitioner at a time when generating theory through research to put into practice was essential. Burt didn't have the benefit of the literature that we drew upon when we entered the profession – a literature that, wonderfully, grows exponentially.

It is important to recall that one of the most famous quotes in psychology conveyed (at least) two meanings. 'There's nothing so practical as a good theory' (Lewin, 1951, p.169) was, first of all, a message to research and applied psychologists to collaborate more effectively because of the mutual benefits, a message that is as apt today; see, for example, Miller and Leyden (1999) and Miller and Frederickson (2006). Second, Lewin was emphasising that as applied psychologists trying to solve challenging problems we ought to look for what theory can tell us to help us with that challenge. It's easy to see why Lewin (1997) became interested in action research and why it has become an attractive method for EPs and other 'real world' researchers.

It is also, therefore, possible to understand what drives the scientist–practitioner. The role that Burt established combined both research and applied psychologist. In just the same way, the contemporary EP ought to combine both in one and the same role. We might add, 'and does so more or less'; however, that requires elaboration and qualification, which we will only skim the surface of here. Indeed, Miller and Frederickson (2006) have teased out the 'struggles and successes for EPs as scientist-practitioners'. Bluntly, it appears to us that it has been much harder to sustain the research role. It can't be because of any lack of the curiosity that must have driven Burt and it can't be (we hope) because the most effective research strategy that anyone requires nowadays is Google – the rot set in before Google was a click away. Rather, something changed in EP professional culture, and to pick up just one of Miller and Frederickson's themes, not least it was the domination of statutory special educational needs work and probably a successive failure of EPs to stake a claim to professional existence based upon what they might offer in terms of research skills as well as anything else. It comes as no surprise, therefore, that the research skills EPs possess aren't necessarily recognised and utilised, in the face of much evidence about the quality and value of the research that EPs do undertake when they have the opportunity.

So, having painted a gloomy picture, why should we be optimistic, which we are? We're optimistic for three reasons. First, a significant strength of the three-year initial training courses is the increased emphasis on research skills, and the accompanying opportunities to realise more fully a scientist–practitioner role. It has to be matched by the opportunities that are provided for trainees as they enter the field. And this leads to our second source of optimism. The research capability of EPs is a role that is recognised and sought when it is fully understood that we offer it. In our respective work bases (a local authority children's services department and a university school of psychology), the research skills that EPs possess aren't necessarily recognised – we have had to communicate about them and demonstrate their value. One of the unexpected benefits of the formation of a children's services department, at least in Hampshire, has been the active desire to develop a research culture, including both the generation of new knowledge through researching what is effective and also how we draw upon the theory and evidence available to influence effective practice.

It is notable that the Children's Workforce Development Council (CWDC) is encouraging small-scale practitioner-led research through funding it, as well as through its occupational group funding providing support for larger scale work. Many EPs have made successful bids to the CWDC. It is also notable that the formerly education research focussed National Foundation for Educational Research is increasingly collaborating with its social care equivalent, Research in Practice (based at Dartington College), and other research partners, manifested not least in the Centre for Excellence in Outcomes (in Children and Young People's services) (CfEO), operational from July 2008. This is clear recognition that the scope and scale of research in Children's Services is shifting away from relatively narrowly drawn boundaries to better reflect the scope of inter-agency work being undertaken and the stronger and stronger imperative to establish effectiveness.

Our third source of optimism takes us to the central purpose of this editorial. In any year it is a matter for celebration that from Burt onwards, EPs have shown an impulse to communicate about their research findings and their work through writing about it and through editing it. In any year it is a matter for celebration that over many decades, what is still a fairly small profession has sustained

two professional publications, the Association of Educational Psychologists' sponsored *Educational Psychology in Practice*, and the Division of Educational and Child Psychology's (DECP) *Educational and Child Psychology*, along with the DECP's quarterly newsletter, *Debate*, which frequently publishes journal-standard articles. This means that some 64 articles are published each year in the two publications and a harder to estimate number of articles, chapters, and books written by EPs are published elsewhere.

In this year, and in this issue of *Educational and Child Psychology*, it is a matter of celebration that the publication has achieved a quarter of a century of volumes. This is an anniversary that the editorial board agreed was essential to mark. There were a number of approaches that we considered, although we appreciated that there was no budget to commission portraits of present and previous editors, and the British Psychological Society could not be persuaded to erect outside their Leicester office a statue of the universal EP unfurling a copy of *Educational and Child Psychology*.

Instead, we drew inspiration from the jury approach to awards that are given to anything from art and architecture to zoos and zoetropes. Our variation of this approach was to advertise and set up panels of three EPs (one panel managed to include a fourth). We were overwhelmed by the numbers of potential volunteers and could have created at least 20 panels. We would like to thank all those who volunteered and in particular those went on to participate.

We selected four articles from each set of three volumes spanning the volumes from 1 (which started in 1983) to 24. We left out the current volume and, regrettably, we decided not to include the issues that appeared under the DECP Occasional Papers series (1972 to 1983). We selected the articles according to somewhat subjective criteria: they said something important at the time about educational psychology practice; they have stood the test of time in that the content has some lasting and so contemporary relevance;

and they are well-written.

This process was, in itself, fascinating. Not surprisingly, it was possible to detect trends in the content of articles as they indicated (then) current trends in and around the profession. There are prolific authors, usually over a defined time period, and authors for whom, so far as we know, it was their first and only published article. There has been an increase in the number of authors who are not EPs but have something to say that is relevant for EP practice. There has also been an increase in the number of authors writing from outside a UK context. Above all, though, and again it wasn't surprising, we were forcibly hit by the depth, quality and range of writing. What was surprising (but perhaps it should not have been) was the number of articles that had stood the test of time; if we hadn't known the date we could easily have assumed that they had been written last week. This meant that whilst our task was enjoyable it was also difficult. We had to make some hard choices to select only four articles.

Correspondingly, we knew that the EP panellists would have a difficult task. Panellists had to confer amongst themselves to determine which one article they would like to select and to write a brief account of why. We asked for this to be about 500 words, a strict discipline that most convenors followed. We debated about editing down the notable exception to this but in the same spirit of supporting diversity that prevented us from banning the fourth panellist, we decided to go with diversity. Overall, we are determined that the exercise of selection is not seen as a case of 'winners' and losers'. The accompanying accounts make it clear that our prediction was correct: panel members had to make a very hard choice, since all four of the articles that they considered could have been reprinted. In this sense, the winner is the quality of the writing and a quality of writing that has endured throughout the life of the publication.

That seems the right point to make in drawing this editorial to its end. This issue celebrates 25 volumes of *Educational and Child Psychology*. We have chosen to celebrate it by drawing attention to the wealth of articles, the commitment of authors, and the care taken by editors. Whether it is explicit or not, in the main the writing in *Educational and Child Psychology* is representative of the scientist–practitioner tradition started by Burt. Even where articles are not written by applied psychologists, the intention is the same: 'There is nothing so practical as a good theory.' Whatever else might be thought or said about 25 years of this publication, the very least that can be said is that even in a digital age, it continues to represent an essential resource for educational psychologists and for psychologists everywhere who share our concerns.

Phil Stringer & Andy Miller

Addresses for correspondence

Dr Phil Stringer, County Services Manager (Educational Psychology, Behaviour Support and School Counselling), Children and Families Branch, Children's Services Department, Ashburton Court East, Winchester, Hampshire SO23 8UG.
E-mail: phil.stringer@hants.gov.uk
Prof. Andy Miller, University of Nottingham, School of Psychology, University Park, Nottingham, NG7 2RD.
E-mail: Andy.Miller@nottingham.ac.uk

References

Lewin, K. (1951). *Field theory in social science; selected theoretical papers.* (Ed. by D. Cartwright.) New York: Harper & Row.

Lewin, K. (1948/1997). Action research and minority groups. In G.W. Lewin & K. Lewin (Eds.) *Resolving social conflicts; selected papers on group dynamics.* Washington, DC: American Psychological Association. New York: Harper & Row.

Miller, A. & Frederickson, N. (2006). Generalisable findings and idiographic problems: Struggles and successes for educational psychologists as scientist-practitioners. In S. Corrie & D. Lane (Eds.) *The modern scientist-practitioner. A guide to practice in psychology.* London: Routledge.

Miller, A. & Leyden, G. (1999). A coherent framework for the application of psychology in schools. *British Educational Research Journal, 25*(3), 389–400.

Volumes 1, 2 and 3 (1984–86): Shortlisted papers

Developing bilingual children's English in schools
by Martin Desforges and Tony Kerr, vol 1(1), 68–80.

Integration: The shadow and the substance
by Peter Mittler, vol 2(3), 8–22.

The use of behaviour modification in the secondary school: A further development
by L.Scott, E. McNamara & E. McPherson, vol 3(1), 4–20.

Routes to partnership with parents: Rhetoric or reality?
by Sheila Wolfendale, vol 3(3), 9–18.

Panel Members
Convenor: Dr Kathie Souter, freelance educational psychologist, Bath
Anne Matthews, senior educational psychologist, Leicestershire
Hugh Watson, educational psychologist, Cambridgeshire

Introduction by the panel

This was a difficult task. Of the four articles selected, and bearing in mind the given criteria, we selected the article by Sheila Wolfendale and the article by Peter Mittler. It was difficult to choose between these two as both convey a sense of history whilst asking questions which are still thought provoking 25 years on. Whilst the panel didn't indicate a strong preference, we selected Wolfendale's by a whisker.

Partnership is a term frequently used in the current practice of educational psychology but how often is the concept merely rhetoric rather than reality? Wolfendale's article sets out to explore a range of perspectives from day-to-day practice to aspirational thinking. The article is accessible and thought-provoking; it challenges views at a theoretical level and promotes active reflection of current practices.

Before examining the concept and role of partnership within practice, Wolfendale identifies a number of areas of change within the professional landscape: all of which continue to challenge practising EPs today. These include the development of an understanding of issues from a systemic perspective; the emphasis on social factors rather than within-child factors; the need to consider the involvement of parents and families; and the importance of developing the necessary skills to deliver psychological services within this reconstruction. The lack of a systematic and rigorous review of practice is highlighted. Wolfendale is scathing in her comments:

> *'…the implicitly sinister undertones of the expert psychologist-passive client mode of casework practice are not even directly tackled in recent critiques of EP practice. (p.9)*

Once again, Wolfendale's comments signal the emergence of a professional stance at odds with the traditional view of the role of the EP as well as the ascendance of evidence based practice.

Having set the scene, the concept of partnership is explored. Wolfendale asserts that partnership is one of a number of key inter-related themes associated with parental involvement. Empowerment, community education and research and evaluation are also identified as important elements when considering 'applied psychological practice in the caring professions'. Wolfendale's emphasis on community education is prophetic in the light of current thinking and initiatives about the changing roles of EPs. Similarly, she is also ahead of her time when highlighting the potential role for EPs in the community to carry out evaluative work.

Finally, the implications for psychological services and how genuine participation can be reflected in daily practice are examined. Examples of joint working with parents and the community are provided; these included multi-agency collaboration. It is proposed that EPs reflect on their own practice. Illustrations of opportunities for parental involvement provide a helpful framework for service review as well as demonstrating how practice has evolved to further involve parents for example, through joint parent-teacher consultation.

In summary, Wolfendale identifies themes and areas for reflection that continue to resonate with practitioners in the 21st century. Educational psychologists are invited to engage in thought and action when considering what psychology can offer to promote a 'curriculum of caring' and identifying appropriate professional skills given the changing context, whilst developing policies and practices that promote involvement.

Kathie Souter, Anne Mathews,
Hugh Watson

Address for correspondence
Kathie Souter, Suite 172, 3 Edgar Buildings, George Street, Bath, BA1 2FJ.
E-mail: kathie@ed-psyk.co.uk

Routes to partnership with parents: Rhetoric or reality?

Sheila Wolfendale, Course tutor, NE London Polytechnic

Very mindful of the theme of the conference (the DECP annual course), I chose a title that I do not intend to tackle or answer head-on; rather, I wish to apply scrutiny to a landscape with which we are all, to a greater or lesser extent, familiar, and to illuminate the issues. I should like to convey a picture of phenomena in transition, and to describe some powerful forces that militate against an easy or simplistic resolution of the question of partnership.

However, I did choose a title that is intended to be expressive of contemporary themes as well as of the inherent uncertainties, and felt, too, that it would be appropriate to deal directly with the role of psychologists, *vis-à-vis* working with parents, and to address, head-on, some of the issues missing in the educational psychology literature.

Looking at the course programme, it is possible to conceptualise a number of differing levels of working with parents, from pragmatic problem-solving to some of the underlying profundities. This is the first mainly EP-focused course-conference that has as its theme 'working with parents'. What does this mean? The importance and relevance of the theme is spelled out by the course organisers in the programme. It is the 'range of perspectives' relevant to psychologists for consideration that I want to pick up and pursue.

It must be thought timely to bring together recent and current thinking and work on parental involvement. I should like to regard my paper as a stock-taking exercise, an audit of where we are at, and what directions we might be moving towards. I should like to range over the following:

- reference to current developments;
- examination of key concepts with
- reference to psychological practice; and
- exploring a case for psychological service policy on parental participation within LEA and community contexts.

The symposia and workshops on this course convey a picture of exciting and diverse work, and represent a significant departure from traditional practice. Which is what?

The assumption is that family work has been a cornerstone of EP practice; that SPSs have been a linchpin between home and school: that family/parental counselling has been a forte, even, some would have said, a *raison d'etre* for EP work. I should like to contend, however, that the traditional EP role in family work has been a jumble of quasi-social work, quasi psychiatry, with an ill-defined, sociopsychological rationale. And, in fact, there is little in the literature on psychologists working in casework contexts to guide us as to requisites for effective casework and the principles on which this might rest. For example, Chazan et al. (1974, chapter 8) offer a totally pragmatic account of working with parents, which concentrates on the interview (home or clinic based) and offer tips as to management and interpretation. It is well-intentioned and benevolent advice, but is exclusively client versus expert-oriented, and does not encompass broader social domains.

The implicitly sinister undertones of the expert psychologist–passive client mode of casework practice are not even directly tackled in recent critiques of EP practice. Whilst these texts address themselves to models of reconstruction, and with some contributors even broadening the base of psychological intervention to include the community, there is no close analysis of requisite professional skills, nor an appraisal of the contribution of the principal actors, the parents and the families.

Thus, although contemporary critiques of traditional practice have kept pace with some changes within socio-educational thinking and concepts of service delivery, nevertheless they do not sufficiently reflect the reconstructed practice of psychologists represented at this course.

I should now like to examine the broader context of contemporary parent-focused and co-operative practice, making a brief reference to current examples of parent-professional work and the rationale. Table I provides a summary of contemporary developments, under these headings:

(a) parents coming into school;
(b) parents as educators;
(c) home-school links;
(d) community education;
(e) parents as governors and managers; and
(f) parents and special needs.

Rationale

The texts in the reference list go· in detail into the ideological base and hypotheses on which many of these initiatives rest. I do not propose to dwell on what is undoubtedly familiar to all of us, save to summarise and list the main strands:

● parents are the child's primary educators;
● combating and compensating for disadvantage;
● maximizing each child's potential;
● utilising and enhancing parental skills;
● ecological perspective;
● empowering parents;
● improving the quality of family life;
● giving expression to parental and consumer rights.

What stands out from this list, what particular hypotheses, what ideology do educational and other practitioner psychologists invoke when they act, when they respond, when they initiate and intervene? Or, to put it another way, what is the legitimacy of the intervention, what guides the psychologists' intrusion into children's and families' lives?

Let us look at some key concepts embedded within the major domains of parental involvement. They are all interrelated and, to my mind, have bearing on applied psychological practice in the caring professions.

1. Partnership

There is no dearth now of definitions and prescriptions for working with parents as partners, rather than as passive client-recipients of services on offer. The books on the 'further reading' list on page 23 offer guiding precepts as means to an end of partnership. Few of us know how that would work in the 'truest' sense, of equal responsibility, equal management, and contractual forms of accountability. But those of us who have had the temerity to define partnership, and who have dabbled with it pragmatically, would also caution against the easy invoking of the word.

For example, Patricia Potts (1983) sees 'partnership' in action currently as a window-dressing, in these words:

'keep parents in the classroom, playroom or sitting room and off the management committee; second, let parents support the work of the professionals rather than question it; third, as parents do not have specialised skills and knowledge to help their children on their own, professional jobs need not be threatened; fourth, working with parents prevents them from organising themselves too well into a separate force and can actually extend the professional role…'

Well, just picking up one implication from this quotation, there *are* parents on Portage management groups, there *are* parents on school governing bodies; there *are* lay citizens as councillors on local education and social services and health committees. But, to extend this representation and to ensure direct opportunities for participation by the 'consumers', should there not be parental representation on management councils of psychological services, education welfare services, area social services, multidiscipli-

Table 1. Major areas of parental involvement in the 1970s and 19805: some examples

---

PARENTS COMING INTO SCHOOL
- helping with reading
- as para-professionals in the classroom

PARENTS AS EDUCATORS AT HOME
- parental involvement in reading, language, maths, learning and 'homework'
- parent-teacher workshops
- Portage
- parent education

HOME-SCHOOL LINKS
- written communication (newsletters) in English and community languages
- moves to open files (NUT policy)
- home-school council (Hargreaves Report recommendation)
- parent-tutor groups (Hargreaves Report recommendations)
- curriculum plans to parents (L.B. Croydon)

COMMUNITY EDUCATION
- parents' room in school
- parents and others attending classes in school
- multidisciplinary work
- local and national parents' associations
- parents' support groups
- LEA community education policy (Coventry, Newham)

PARENTS AS GOVERNORS AND MANAGERS
- parent governors
- parents on nursery and playgroup management

PARENTS AND SPECIAL NEEDS
- parental involvement in referral
- parental involvement in assessment, including Section 5, and reviews
- parental involvement in parents' associations
- parental involvement in behaviour & learning programmes
- parents' association

---

nary child development and district handicap teams? Can the maintenance of professional bulwarks, the defence behind what Midwinter (1977) described as 'a barricade of mystiques' be justified by those who erected them in the first place? Midwinter further claimed that we professionals are 'jittery about evelation and open accountabil-ity, jargon-plagued and status-conscious'. These factors do somewhat militate against a gratuitous, cosy notion of partnership and, after all, the very term 'service delivery' could imply at worst colonial overtones and betray origins in Christian charity and do-gooding, rather than in scientific precepts.

Gliedman and Roth (1981) assert that

parents should oversee and orchestrate the services that professionals for provide their children. Their thesis continues:

'parents of all races and social classes should be able to pick and choose among different experts, obtain outside opinions when dissatisfied with the services or advice provided by a professional, and constantly evaluate the professional's performance in terms of the overall needs of the growing child' (p.235)

'many professionals find it natural to believe that they are experts about the kinds of values that parents should possess and inculcate in their children. Much of the conflict and confusion that occurs between parents and professionals in handicap stems from the almost self-evident character of the professional's intuitive feeling that he is a moral expert as well as a technical expert' (p.236).

However, my rejoinder to that blow is that we may be put into the position of appearing to be moral arbiters precisely *because* the relationship between professional and parent-as-client was never perceived to be one in which complementary expertise was shared.

The managerial role that Gliedman and Roth believe parents should play brings us to another key concept.

2. Empowerment

Bruner it was, I think, who used the term 'the felt powerlessness' of the disadvantaged in society, who have no access to inform, to make and affect decisions. But all of us, at some time, feel powerless against professional and trade guilds, and the vested interests of any monopoly. Recent attention to 'powersharing' by parents (as 'clients', as consumers) has been based on the premise that they do have the right to be directly involved in decision-making about their own children. In a broader societal context, citizens have a direct right to be involved in some decision-making that affects *them*: a *process* involvement rather than just an intermittent ballot-box involvement.

'Empowerment' has been defined as 'a process through which people become more able to influence those people and organisations that affect their lives and the lives of those they care about'. Here is a fuller definition from a chapter in a recently published book, *Child Psychology in Action: linking research and practice*, edited by John Harris(1986):

'an interactive process involving mutual respect and critical reflection through which people and controlling institutions are changed in ways which provide those people with greater influence over individuals and institutions which are in some way impeding their efforts to achieve equal status in society, for themselves and those they care about' (p.15).

This chapter by Moncrieff Cochrane goes on to describe the Family Matters programme initiated by himself and Urie Bronfenbrenner in the late 1970s. As an intervention programme, it departed from the 'deficit family' model inherent in earlier Head Start, etc., projects and invoked the following starting points:

● that the ecological perspective is the crucial underpinning to any family focused programme;

● that parents are experts on their own children;

● that there are already lodged within and between families much knowledge and wisdom about childrearing and existing resources;

● that parents should be the determinants and the deciders of family life.

The findings are reported in the chapter. Of special relevance to this discussion was the realisation that empowerment was a gradual process, evolving over time, change in people's self-perception, growth in confidence that they could get things done, influence, even control events. The chapter concludes with comments pertaining to 'programmes for families' and service delivery.

Might one of the aims of EPs for child-focused intervention, whether in a systems or individualised framework, be parental empowerment? Cochrane queries whether the goal of service provision is 'to foster independent, self-supporting individuals and families' (p.29). If this is so, should a systems approach explicitly incorporate or even be defined by ecological models that demonstrate the power of community networks that we ignore at our peril? What that could mean in practical terms is that we utilize the idea of eco-mapping for each child, carefully analyse the networks that are revealed by such an exercise, and plan our intervention accordingly.

3. Community education

Community education could be regarded as an umbrella to many initiatives and a living expression of a number of rationales to involving parents. It may be that educational and community psychologists have rather lagged behind initiatives in their own localities, perhaps have not been invited in, perhaps have not been perceived as relevant, perhaps have themselves regarded their work within remedial and special contexts as peripheral.

But it would be consistent within an EP's job description and brief to be involved in the promotion of equal opportunities and an integrated approach to educational provision (e.g. London Borough of Newham's *Going Community* document), preventive intervention, parent support, parent education, parent classes and workshops, parental involvement in reading, literacy, maths and learning.

Already many psychologists are involved with such initiatives, but rarely within an overall LEA and community strategy. Input needs to move from being fragmented to being part of a coherent contribution to LEA policy on matters of current concern within the community, such as equal opportunities, anti-racist practice and integration; last year's DECP course proceedings amply demonstrate how centrally placed the EP is in effecting policy into practice, published as *Educational and Child Psychology*, 2(3), 1985,

'Integration: possibilities, practice and pitfalls'.

Just before Christmas the House of Lords was to debate community education, which a small but increasing number of LEAs are adopting. The idea of 'lifelong learning', reduction of the barriers between school as a place where learning takes place, and community where the 'real' life goes on, has clear implications for all who work with and within schools.

4. Research and evaluation

Roy McConkey (1986) in *Child Psychology in Action* (Harris, 1986) takes a visionary look at how service-based research might be developed which will be characterised by the following elements.

(a) A commitment to developing both the policy and the practices of the services to which they belong. This will entail regular monitoring of clients' needs along with short- and long-term evaluation of services provided.

(b) An involvement in developing the skills of staff and parents, so that new insights can be translated into ongoing practice in the negotiated manner advocated by Bruner.

(c) The collection and analysis of objective and accurate information regarding particular problems facing the service will inform the development of solutions. Such data may have to be culled from census returns, economic reports, retrospective analysis of clients' records and opinion poll type surveys (pp.246-7).

Psychologists in the community are eminently placed to carry out evaluative work and there is encouraging evidence that this is increasingly built into intervention programmes, whether school or home focused. In the context of this paper and the theme of working with parents, there is so much scope for participant research, for data collection to be rooted within and emanate from the processes of parent-child interaction, and parent-child-professional contact. Two examples of parent-focused clinical research might illuminate this point: Hilton Davis' work on the child characterization sketch (Cunningham & Davis, 1985) and the work on parental profiling in chapter 17 of the same book.

Perhaps we can evolve towards a formulation of research needs jointly worked out by all participants which gets away from the 'top down' imposition of prior-defined problems towards a 'street level' appraisal of problem-solving strategies, in which those in receipt of all sorts of community services ranging from street-cleaning, parks maintenance and provision of health services have a say in those provisions. That includes all of us. An interesting initiative is the joint project between the Consumer Council and Newcastle City Council in which ratepayers and house-holders were to be asked their views on the frequency and adequacy of the refuse collection and also their views on what they wanted in their parks. As Teresa Smith has put it (in Henderson et al., 1980) within a community work context 'it should be local people themselves who define what is to be defined as 'change' and what is not' (p.224).

The take-up of an 'open door', a 'drop-in' facility provided by a psychological or child guidance or social services based at a local school or community centre may reflect the perceived need by consumers which could be a more accurate index of what they want than the controlled filtering of formal referral procedures and the static nature of a waiting list.

Evaluation then rightfully incorporates techniques that allow for the views and perceptions of service receivers to have equal weight and to complement other forms of product evaluation. An example of an evaluation which is process as well as product focused, which draws heavily on the evolving written and verbal views of the project participants, is the Family Services Unit Report on a London-based Home School Liaison venture (McCreadie, 1985).

Implications for psychological services

I maintained at the outset of this paper that in family-focused work there had been inade-

quate consideration of what I termed socio-psychological principles. I have sought to demonstrate how a rationale could be constructed for working with families and within the community which is validly predicated on principles that owe little to pathology and deficit models but owe much to notions of citizen's rights and the differential skills, or 'equivalent expertise' of all members of a caring society.

Perhaps 'individual casework' spurned by more recent recruits to the profession for being pathology-driven as well as being time-consuming, takes on renewed significance when children and their parents are involved as problem-definers, decision-makers, designers of their own problem-solving approaches. In a spirit of parent-professional partnership, Peter Mittler (Mittler & McConachie, 1983) talked of 'goal plans' for various levels and types of participation which equally involves parents in sharing responsibility for outcomes, for they will have been intimately involved in all stages of problem formulation and problem resolution.

I referred just a moment ago to 'differential skills' and 'equivalent expertise'. Rather more attention has focused on 'giving psychology away' than on a dynamic notion of professional skill maintenance and enhancement. Roy McConkey sees skills development as being integral to professional practice. Prerequisites to working effectively with parents in non-traditional ways are means of professional self-appraisal and skills analysis (to be explored in the 1981 Act symposium). Some, but not enough preparation is given to this developing role, as it can be assumed that prior casework-type experience is sufficient. That it is not – and certainly not for the demands now placed upon psychologists – is attested to by the suggestions made by parents' groups that gave evidence to the Fish Committee as to the kind of skills training they felt they needed and that professionals needed, to work with them. The lists in Fish of these training needs would make a sound basis for local parental and professional in-service training.

In the final part of my paper I wish to propose that it would be consistent with contemporary thinking as described, for psychological services to have a written policy on parental involvement, which demonstrates how psychological services can have impact at all levels; that they have much expertise to contribute that is more pervasive than contexts of referral and 'treatment' might suggest. Services that are familiar with the setting of aims and objectives for EP practice may not baulk at the idea of producing major policy statements on issues of local and national concern that affect their practice directly, such as equal opportunities, integration, anti-racism and parental and community involvement.

Policy into practice might look like table 2.

If this were a workshop rather than a formal talk I would be asking you to formulate SPS policy from the areas of involvement sketched out in table 2. It would be tempting but presumptuous for me to do so, for the uniqueness of your own settings and your

Table 2. Psychological services: working with parents and the community (including joint work with schools and agencies)

AREA OF INVOLVEMENT	SELECTED EXAMPLES
Individual: child) family) (a) assessment + statementing	Joint referrals Home visiting Open door/drop in Parental profiling + parental contribution Open reporting Parents at case conferences
(b) intervention + programmes	Parental involvement in reading, maths, learning Behaviour management Portage Counselling, family therapy Parent support workshops and courses
School and community education	INSET courses and workshops Formulation of parental involvement policy Talking with governors and governor training Parent education, parent training
LEA and education committee	Participation in policy formulation Review an evaluation of provision INSET planning and provision Report to committees on family and community work (annual review of aims and objectives) Involvement in grant applications

Community	Psychological service advertising and publicity
	    (shops, markets)
	Community locus for groups and workshops
	Contributions to social audit and social planning of
	    provision (nurseries, play-space recreation needs)
	Social learning, routes to coping support

particularly local concerns would be reflected in your policy statements if they were truly representative.

To end I invite you to share the vision of Urie Bronfenbrenner (in Zigler et al., 1983) who puts forward a new paradigm for child and family policy, thus:

'the need is to create formal systems of challenge and support that generate and strengthen informal systems of challenge and support, that in turn reduce the need for the formal systems' (p.405).

He names three principal sources that offer the 'most powerful and promising counter-active strategies', namely 'the school, the family's social networks, and the parents' world of work'. Amongst his 'five preposterous proposals', he advocates a 'curriculum of caring' in our schools, and the enhancement of parent empowerment through the creation of supportive social networks.

In short, and in conclusion, what Bronfenbrenner and others have advocated is a national policy on children: for their welfare and with the best support systems that we are currently capable of devising and sustaining. These aspirations transcend routes to partnership. Partnership with parents, perhaps a laudable, even achievable, aim, itself would be taking us further along the route to ensuring 'a fairer future for children'.

References

Chazan, M., Moore, T., Williams, P. & Wright, J. (1974). *The practice of educational psychology.* London: Longmans

Cunningham, C. & Davis, H. (1985). *Working with parents: Frameworks for collaboration.* Milton Keynes: Open University Press

Gliedman, J. & Roth, W. (1981). Parents and professionals. In W. Swann (Ed.) *The practice of special education.* Oxford: Basil Blackwell and Open University Press

Harris, J. (1986). *Child psychology in action: Linking research and practice.* London: Croom Helm (and reference to chapters by Cochrane and McConkey).

Midwinter, E. (1977) The professional-lay relationship: A Victorian legacy. *Journal of Child Psychology and Psychiatry, 18*(2), 101–113.

Potts, P. (1983). What difference would integration make to the professionals? In T. Booth & P. Potts (Eds) *Integrating special education.* Oxford: Blackwell.

Henderson, P., Jones, D. & Thomas, D. (Eds.) (1980). *The boundaries of change in community work.* London: George Allen &. Unwin

McCreadie, C. (1985). *Home school liaison: Report of an experimental project in community work.* London: Family Service Units.

Mittler, P. & McConachie, H. (Eds.) (1983). *Parents, professialals and mentally handicapped people.* Beckenham: Croom Helm.

Zigler, L., Kagan, S. & Klugman, E. (Eds.) (1983). *Children, families and government.* Cambridge: Cambridge University Press.

Further reading:

Selected texts on parental involvement with particular reference to work in the UK.

Cullingford, C. (Ed.) (1985). Parents, teachers and schools. London: Robert Royce.

Hargreaves, D. (Chairperson) (1984). *Improving secondary schools.* London: ILEA

Volumes 4, 5 and 6 (1987–89): Shortlisted papers

The educational psychologist and primary prevention: Well matched or 'shotgun wedding'
by Peter Hamilton, vol 4(2), 5–13.

Training for the role of school consultant as a means of dealing effectively with behaviour problems in schools
by Carol Aubrey, vol 4(2), 14–29.

Educational psychologists working in multicultural communities: An analysis
by Trevor Bryans, vol 5(2), 8–18.

A school consultation service
by Joan Figg and Rob Stoker, vol 6(3), 34–42.

Panel Members
Convenor: Tom Lowe, senior educational psychologist, North Lanarkshire
Charlie Gow, educational psychologist, North Lanarkshire
Laura Walmsley, educational psychologist, North Lanarkshire

Introduction by the panel

The three of us are based in the same service and, indeed, in the same centre. When looking at the four articles, we soon realised that we came to them from differing perspectives but with a shared Scottish orientation. Tom and Charlie lived through the period of 're-constructing educational psychology' in the 1980s. These and similar articles formed part of their early reading and professional history. Laura, on the other hand, has very recently qualified. For her, this literature is part of the history of educational psychology. Scotland has long had a different educational system from the rest of the UK, which is reflected in the nature of the educational psychology services here. Central to current practice and thinking is the *Review of Provision of Educational Psychology Services in Scotland* (Scottish Executive, 2002; the 'Currie Report' after its chairperson) which presented educational psychology services with many challenges for the future delivery of educational psychology and set our practice within a matrix framework of five core functions delivered across three key levels. Furthermore, while the issues of the inclusion of members of different nationalities and cultures has been much less an issue here than elsewhere, it has been brought into sharp focus recently by a further influx of East Europeans, primarily from Poland, and the immigration of a large group of refugees from the Democratic Republic of the Congo.

In each of the four articles, we could identify issues that resonated with the contexts and challenges that we are experiencing today and ideas that remain relevant today. However, we quickly settled on two articles from which to make our final choice. We have to admit to struggling with the aggressive tone of Trevor Bryan's article in which we read that he was accusing us, as white educational psychologists, with, what we would now label as, 'institutional racism'.

Yet, once less defensive, we fully endorsed many of his recommendations, for example, the level of ethnic representation in our services, the need to be alert to our personal values, and the temptation and danger in becoming an agent of the dominant group.

After a period of discussion of the pros and cons of the four articles, Hamilton's articulation of the importance and our role in primary prevention emerged as the one that we wanted to select to represent this particular set of volumes of *Educational and Child Psychology*. Our decision was helped by its clarity and accessible structure. The key points which pushed it to the front came from its continuing insights and relevance over 20 years. He outlines 'levels of intervention' which our Currie Report 'rediscovered' and the enduring value of a mix of approaches focusing on individuals and those requiring more systemic activities. Similarly, he addresses the process of achieving change in organisations, highlighting that it is an 'implementation-dominated process' and our role is to refuse to offer 'expert-type' solutions but should facilitate others to develop their skills and solutions. If written today, his exploration of the skills and strategies required of educational psychologist to effect change would be as accurate and powerfully compelling.

Tom Lowe, Charlie Gow, Laura Walmsley

Reference

Scottish Executive (2002). *Review of provision of educational psychology services in Scotland* (The Currie Report). Edinburgh: Scottish Executive.

Address for correspondence

Tom Lowe, Senior Psychologist, Psychological Service, Sikeside Street, Coatbridge, ML5 4QH.
E-mail: tom.lowe@ea.n-lanark.sch.uk

The educational psychologist and primary prevention: Well matched or a 'shotgun wedding'

Peter Hamilton, Western Australia Education Department

A T THE RISK of oversimplifying the diversity of opinion regarding how the educational psychologist can best contribute to education, three groups can be discerned. The first group would say that the increasing emphasis on preventive services and the profile of skills of the educational psychologist point to a happy union of the two. The second group would acknowledge the need for educational psychologists to be less involved with crisis-oriented services and more concerned with problem prevention, but would see this trend chiefly as a response to disillusionment with traditional service provision rather than their training and expertise equipping them to play such a role. A third group perhaps do not see any need to change from the traditional direct service model which has characterised the profession to date. After a long period of wooing primary prevention, the first group of practitioners are often frustrated that it is taking so long to get to the altar; the second group are mostly anxious about whether they will be up to the task when they do get there; and the third group are too busy testing to get to the wedding.

The aims of this paper are:

(a) to be fairly specific about the skills required of an educational psychologist to successfully design and implement a primary prevention programme;

(b) to suggest some ways in which the educational psychologists' involvement in primary prevention programmes might be promoted.

The material which informs the position taken here is from recent developments in the Western Australian Education Department where educational psychologists have been active in this work. Before turning to the details of such work, some clarification of the nature of primary prevention is offered.

Levels of intervention

Caplan's (1970) conceptualisation of three levels of intervention helps to clarify how the term primary prevention is used here.

1. Primary prevention efforts are designed for large numbers of people before the fact of disorder. They have healthy people as their targets with the aim of building psychological health and resources in them.

2. Secondary preventions aim at high-risk children or people whose problems are just starting. Early identification and intervention belong here.

3. Tertiary prevention services intervene with already established problems, the goal is to repair the damage so the person can function in their natural environment.

A comprehensive approach to service provision involves interventions at each level (Clarizio, 1979). Educational psychologists have been predominantly involved in tertiary level services with increasing movement into secondary level programmes. Examples of attempts at true primary prevention programmes are relatively rare and evidence of successful ones even rarer. Cowan (1980) has identified several types of primary prevention activities, but for those of us interested in schools there are two major kinds of preventive endeavour.

1. Competence training, where educational programmes are designed to

teach specific competencies that are thought to mediate positive adjustment: an example of this approach is the interpersonal problem-solving training work of Spirack et al. (1976) and the use of materials such as *Steps to Success* (Thacker, 1982).

2. Intervening to change the social environment of the school: given that the school is a high-impact social environment that significantly shapes the individual's psychological development, attempts at changing the mainstream policies and practices of the organisation have emerged. Examples of successful school-based programmes of this sort are difficult to find; what one more commonly encounters is a comprehensive logging of the nature of schools as organisations which make such interventions problematic (Sarason, 1971). The adage 'the more things change the more they remain the same' is offered by Kerr (1984) as an apt summary of the outcomes of much of the work in this area. The Rochester Primary Mental Health Project (Cowan et al., 1975) and the Connecticut Behaviourally Oriented Multilevel Preventive Approach (Allen et al., 1976) are exceptions. Recent work in Western Australia has also produced some promising results in generating schoolwide reform.

The Western Australian project

The problem of disruptive secondary school students knows no national boundaries, and was of such concern to the Western Australian Education Department that in 1982 a decision was made to allocate resources to assist schools with the problem. The programme which resulted came to be known as 'Managing student behaviours: a whole school approach' and was introduced into selected secondary schools in 1983. The programme continues to operate in its fourth year with over 40 participating schools in that period.

I. Programme design

The position taken from Burden (1978), Gillham (1981), Galloway et al. (1982), Leach (1981) and Hargreaves (1978) was that preventive action for problems at school is best taken at the level of the classroom management skills of the individual teacher, and at the level of the school as an organisation. The shape of the programme reflects these twin emphases by beginning with an intensive in-service course for a core group of teachers in classroom management skills, followed by an extended consultation stage in which a school discipline policy was developed based on the involvement of the whole school community, both in its development and implementation. During this stage the consultant uses a collaborative problem-solving process to engage the school in reviewing its current practices, isolating and defining problems, developing alternative approaches based on the principles of effective management, clarifying roles and communication channels, and monitoring progress towards its goals. In this process school ownership of the programme is maximised and fundamental changes in the ethos of the school made possible through teachers working collaboratively, decisions being made participatively and problems being approached with a problem-solving orientation.

The design of the programme is built around developing a strategically composed core group of teachers as a 'critical mass' for the change effort. The in-service course generates in the group a belief in the efficacy of the school in changing the behaviour of the students, a commitment to a set of effective management principles, an acknowledgement of the need to develop both within-class strategies and out-of-class support structures, a determination to involve the whole school in decisions about the system to be implemented, and a resolve to build into the system ongoing professional development opportunities for staff to continually expand their expertise in this area.

2. Programme implementation

The literature on school reform has given one message loud and clear: that the outcomes of a change effort depend critically on how it is implemented, i.e. that change is an implementation-dominated process and more attention needs to be paid to how programmes get implemented rather than on their objective merits. As Berman and McLaughlin (1978) have observed: 'The quality of an innovation (as deemed by experts) is not a predictor of its ultimate use' (p.161). It is hoped that this lesson was learned in Western Australia and particular attention was given to this stage of the project. The skills which are required to carry it off are considered in some detail in the next section.

Implementation proceeded through the following stages:

(a) initial contracting with school management;

(b) delivery of the in-service course for a core group of staff;

(c) consultation with the whole school during the policy development phase;

(d) ongoing consultation and training during the policy implementation phase.

It will be immediately obvious that we are dealing here with an extended time-scale; although the in-service course is completed within a few months, the consultation stages will demand an involvement over a much longer period. Fullan (1982) reminds us that change programmes of this sort should be thought of in terms of a two- to three-year timescale and our work would support this.

The implementation of the programme also takes into account some other aspects of the literature on educational change that relate to implementation success. Central amongst these is the critical importance of leadership in the school. Both the Principal and the Deputy Principal are written into all stages of the programme so that their support is active and visible. They are participants in the initial negotiations about the goals of the programme, the commitment involved and organisational arrangements. They are also compulsory members of the in-service group and expected to complete the homework between sessions. This provides the basis for their continued engagement during the policy development stage and hopefully the commitment to build in the long-term supports for the school's discipline system, i.e. budget items, timetabling provision, recognition of staff, and all the other activities that demonstrate to staff that the management values the approach being implemented.

Another recurring theme in the literature is the importance of school ownership of the programme if implementation is to be sustained (Johnson, 1985). So many innovations are owned by those who design them and take them into schools. They then expect high fidelity implementation of their programme and expend much energy in persuading teachers to oblige. This scenario is usually concluded by complaints about how resistant to change the teachers are and how poor the school is at incorporating innovations. Berman and McLaughlin (1976) have emphasised the need for 'mutual adaptation' to occur if innovations are to survive beyond the very short term.

In the 'Managing student behaviour: a whole school approach' programme each school uses the programme to suit their own needs. The consultant must be satisfied with approximations of what he or she would like to see in place. If school ownership is taken seriously then those in the school must develop their discipline system and this may not coincide with what the educational psychologist feels would best suit their needs. The danger here, of course, is that in the process of adaptation, all those aspects which involve any real change will be eliminated and only the safe, non-threatening 'changes' will be implemented. How much challenge the school is able to sustain before retreating to a defensive posture will be a reflection of its stage of development and this must be respected by the consultant.

3. Programme evaluation

A range of measures were taken in the eight secondary schools who first participated in the programme during 1984. Various indices of each school's operation were taken prior to its inclusion in the programme, during the year that the school participated in the programme, and a year after the programme. There were clear indications that, overall, these schools made significant changes in the direction of what has been identified in the literature as the characteristics of effective schools. They showed reductions in the use of corporal punishment, they produced discipline policies with whole school involvement, they had significant reductions in the numbers of students referred to deputy principals for disciplinary action, teachers reported feeling less stressed, teachers perceived large reductions in disruptive behaviour in the classroom and tended to attribute disruptive behaviour to factors within the school which could be solved rather than out of school factors which could not be controlled.

While there is no claim that the programme is a panacea to the problem of student disruption, there is evidence that the schools who participate do make substantial changes and maintain these changes with minimal outside support. Hamilton (1986) provides a full description of the measures used and results obtained.

Skills of the educational psychologist

In attempting to change the organisational climate of a large secondary school as the 'Managing student behaviour: a whole school approach' programme does, a diverse range of skills is required. The main contention of this paper is that the educational psychologist can provide such expertise. The following three areas are proposed as crucial skill clusters for successfully designing, implementing and evaluating such a programme.
1. A common feature of the design, implementation and evaluation of the programme is the adoption of a 'systems' perspective at all levels of the intervention.
   (a) At the classroom level
   In working with teachers during the inservice course stage, it was seen as vital to couch the problem of misbehaving students in terms of the system of interactions in the classroom between teachers and students, students and students, students and tasks, rather than in terms of a student-owned problem. Viewing misbehaviour as a product of the set of classroom interactions also takes the blame out of the issue, i.e. either blaming students (as teachers may want to do) or blaming teachers for the problem (which is unlikely to get a favourable response). Such a perspective thus facilitates an examination of the teacher's role and orientates teachers to a wider view of the problem.
   (b) At the school level
   Having an understanding of the school as a social system is fundamental to developing whole school approaches. Intervening in any subsystem of the school, e.g the discipline system, a particular group of teachers, will have effects on other subsystems, e.g. the pastoral care system, the leadership. The consultant will need to acknowledge the interrelationships amongst these subsystems if schoolwide support systems are to be developed for both students and staff.
   (c) At the education department level
   Schools do not operate in isolation either, and taking account of the wider context in which the school functions (particularly the relationship between schools and the Education Department) is necessary. A key factor in the design of the programme was the analyses of the wider system concerns existing at the time. These centred around the following:
   (i) concern to develop alternatives to corporal punishment;
   (ii) increased accountability of schools in the light of recent legislation allowing for permanent removal of students from school;
   (iii) increasing publicity of teacher stress as being a widespread problem.

Having these issues clearly identified at the beginning of the programme enabled appropriate decisions to be made about how to structure the intervention, who to communicate with during implementation and how to express the outcomes.

2. The INSET component of the programme is integral to the process of whole school change and requires both an understanding of the literature on classroom management and, most importantly, the skills of group leadership. In terms of content, there are many resources to draw upon. There is an extensive behavioural literature (e.g . Sulzer-Azaroff & Mayer, 1977), packaged programmes such as Teacher Effectiveness Training (Gordon, 1974), Systematic Training for Effective Teaching (Dinkmeyer & McKay, 1979) and the Ten Step Discipline Programme (Glasser, 1976).

Unfortunately, the group leadership skills cannot be acquired in the same way and yet, if the in-service group is to form a cohesive core group providing the impetus for change, the success of the group leader in being able to build such a group climate will be critical. Anyone who has sat down with a group of 15 or so teachers drawn widely from a large secondary school and attempted to develop such a shared perspective will know it is not easy. The group leader needs to be alert to recognising contributions by group members, listening empathically, summarising emerging themes, linking contributions, and dealing with resistance expressed and unexpressed. This latter skill needs to be elaborated because it goes to the heart of facilitating collaboration between teachers which underlies the programme.

Many a group leader is undone by the resistant group member who is critical of others, negative about change proposals, and undermining of efforts towards co-operative work. The temptation is to try and eliminate the resistance so that progress can be made, or ignore it and hope it will go away. Neither option produces the desired result. Incorporating resistance in group solutions not only allows the resistors to be included in the group, it also enhances the quality of group solutions.

The teacher who, in discussions about what the school can do to manage disruptive students, argues that they should be sent home and their parents told to deal with them, may not immediately appear to be making a useful contribution and yet if such a position can be reframed by the group leader to a statement about the school needing to be clear about drawing a line where its responsibility stops, i. e. boundary setting, then it represents a positive contribution to constructive problem-solving. Similarly the teacher who asserts that 'pupils who misbehave need to be given a good thrashing; that's what they understand', is in fact making a statement about the importance of effective sanctions if behaviour exceeds the limits set. When reframed in this way such a statement leads to a follow-on discussion about what limits, what sanctions, how to judge whether sanctions are effective or not, etc. The resistor has a positive function in drawing the group's attention to dimensions of the problem which may otherwise escape consideration.

By persistently refusing to offer expert-type solutions to problems generated by the teachers, and insisting that teachers have the resources to solve such difficulties, responsibility is kept where it belongs: with them. By working in such a fashion the group leader also avoids what Sarason (1971) describes as the trap of treating teachers in precisely the same way as teachers are criticised for treating their students, i.e. simply telling them what to do. It is also consistent with the proposition consistently supported in the educational change literature (Kerr, 1984): that teachers learn best from other teachers. The educational psychologist's skill is in creating the conditions necessary for this to happen. The woefully inadequate peer support systems in schools testify to the fact that such conditions do not occur naturally.

3. Once a cohesive core group is established through the application of the process skills described above, the next step is to build outwards to include the rest of the staff and this requires additional skills from the educational psychologist. At this stage of the programme the role of the educational psychologist shifts from being facilitator of a small group, to that of a problem-solving consultant to the whole school, as the core group sets about including, motivating and educating others. The myriad of problems that occur during this period of forming comittees, allocating tasks, surveying needs, writing policies, and the like, need to be approached with a problem-solving orientation. The educational psychologist's capacity to continue to model and teach such a perspective in the variety of situations that emerge is crucial to the successful ownership and resolution of the problems by the school. The temptation to revert to a dependent 'ask the expert' or a counterdependent 'it can't be done, you try and make us' position, will be particularly strong amongst the staff and the commitment of the consultant to remain in the role of a problem-solving consultant will be keenly tested.

Staff divisions will very likely emerge with an issue as contentious as the management of disruptive behaviour, and it will be hard for core-group teachers to remain non-defensive and concentrate on problems being expressed rather than the people who are expressing them. The skills of the educational psychologist in acknowledging this frustration but continuing to work to clarify problems, encourage people to generate solutions, consider consequences of different courses of action, make plans for the implementation of decisions made, and build in evaluation of outcomes, are required if the programme is to survive this transition stage.

The participants in this exercise will be immersed in the system and often unable to see how decisions regarding one aspect of the school's operation will reverberate throughout the system. The educational psychologist will need to have an eye to the total system and continually place on the agenda for the school the need to safeguard threatened parts of the system and acknowledge the differing needs of those occupying particular positions in the school.

Since one of the major objectives of the programme is to assist the school in devising their discipline policy, the consultant also needs to have a working knowledge of the stages of policy development. Addressing questions of structure before issues of rationale have been resolved is an example of how schools' inexperience with policy development can create unnecessary confusion. While the consultant does not direct the stages to be worked through, sensitising those involved by asking the right questions at the right time can help the school to maximise the return for the effort expounded.

Making the shift to prevention

Educational psychologists are not often invited to drop everything and mount primary prevention programmes. Any movements in this direction are usually achieved only after much struggling to re-educate people about a more useful role. In this section some consideration will be given to how the prospects of educational psychologists becoming involved in such work might be improved. Three principles emerge from the Western Australian programme which are relevant to this.

1. Educational psychologists need to relate their prevention programmes to the current mainstream issues in education. There is no doubt that the issue of disruptive students is alive and kicking in many secondary schools and it might be claimed that a problem which is of crisis proportions is difficult to approach with a longer-term preventive focus, that teachers will want immediate relief from the most difficult cases and this will militate against taking a broader and longer-term perspective. Indeed the problem could be tackled at each of the levels described earlier, i.e. a tertiary-level intervention would target the students who are proving the greatest headache and attempt to reduce the extent of their disruptiveness; a secondary prevention programme would identify the 'at risk' students or those in the early stages of their deviant careers and seek to change the course of the development of the problem; a primary prevention programme would aim to change the mainstream practice of schools which contribute to the maintenance of the problem. The point is that by tackling a problem which is keenly and immediately felt at the school level, it is possible to negotiate with staff a broader brief involving preventive approaches, providing the focus on the most pressing problems is not disregarded entirely.

2. Educational psychologists need to be more active in demonstrating how their expertise is appropriate to the resolution of current educational issues. If we take the concept of 'whole school' policies as an example, there appears to be little recognition of what educational psychologists might have to offer in this area. Schools are being urged in various educational reports to adopt whole school approaches to literacy, assessment, guidance, pastoral care, discipline, equal opportunity, and numerous other areas of the school's operation with little acknowledgement of all that is involved in that recommendation. By showing how complex such a proposition is, involving as it does collaboration, shared decision making, conflict resolution, problem solving, and the like, and relating their skills to those needs, the services of the educational psychologist may be seen in a different light.

The larger issue involved here is the naive assumption underlying such recommendations that change is a decision or an event, i.e. that knowing a whole school approach is required, the school can simply decide to adopt it. Change is a process, and for its implementation requires expertise of the sort the educational psychologist can provide. This message needs to be given to those who allocate resources: that if we want more than just the appearance of change, serious consideration should be given to the kind of support service required. This is not the same as suggesting a public relations exercise to promote the usefulness of educational psychologists in facilitating change. What is being advocated here is to take critical educational issues of the day, analyse and dissect them, and be quite implicit and specific about how the educational psychologist can contribute to their resolution.

3. Educational psychologists need to be sensitive to the culture of schools. One of the major reasons why the programme discussed here has maintained its support is that in its design it addresses the central features of the culture of schools that create problems for both the people who teach in them (who want some sense of achievement, recognition, development and growth, stimulation, and social satisfaction), and those who support schools (who want them to be responsive, self-critical and self-renewing organisations).

Such characteristics as professional isolation, lack of recognition by bureaucratic structures, dependence on punishment as the major control mechanism, poor linkages between different levels of the organisation, lack of consensus about goals, poorly monitored operations, and lack of a problem-solving approach, will all be familiar to those who have close contact with secondary schools. It is likely that the interest and enthusiasm generated by the programme stems not simply from its impact on student behaviour but from the fact that it is impinging on the organisational climate of the school with increasing satisfaction for those who work in it. Programmes which take cognisance of these factors, both in their design and implementation, can be expected to enjoy increased support.

Conclusion

The skills required successfully to carry out primary prevention programmes, such as the 'Managing student behaviour: a whole school approach' programme in Western Australia, are different from those exercised by educational psychologists working in the traditional model. An attempt has been made here to capture the nature of that difference. Given that these skills are in short supply in the education system at a time when change is being widely advocated, it is to be hoped that educational psychologists will create opportunities to demonstrate their usefulness in these ways.

References

Allen, G.J., Chinsky, J.M., Lockman, J.E. & Sellinger, H.V. (1976). *Community psychology in the schools: A behaviourally oriented multilevel preventive approach.* Hillsdale, NJ: Lawrence Erlbaum Associates.

Berman, P. & McLaughlin, M. (1976). Implementation of educational innovation. *Educational Forum, 40*(3), 345–370.

Berman, P. & McLaughlin, M. (1978). *Designing implementation to match policy situation: A contingency analysis of programmed and adaptive implementation.* Santa Monica, CA: Rand Corp.

Burden, R.L. (1978) Schools' systems analysis: A project centred approach. In B. Gillham (Ed.) *Reconstructing educational psychology.* London: Croom Helm.

Caplan, G. (1970). *The theory and practice of mental health consultation.* New York: Basic Books.

Clarizio, A.F. (1979). Primary prevention of behavioural disorders in the schools. *School Psychology Review, 8*(4), 434–445.

Cowan, E.L. (1980). The wooing of primary prevention. *American Journal of Community Psychology, 8*, 258–284.

Cowan, E.L., Trost, M.A., Lorion, R.P., Dorr, D., Izzo, L.D. & Issacson, R.V. (1975). *New ways in school mental health: Early detection and prevention of school maladaptation.* New York: Human Science Press, Inc.

Dinkmeyer, D. & McKay, G. (1979) Systematic training for effective teaching.

Fullan, M. (1982). *The meaning of educational change.* New York: Teachers College Press.

Galloway, D., Ball, T., Blomfield, O. & Seyd, R. (1982). *Schools and disruptive pupils.* Longman: London.

Gillham, B. (1981). *Problem behaviours in the secondary school.* London: Croom Helm.

Glasser, W. (1976). *The ten step discipline programme.* Educator Training.

Gordon, T. (1974) Teacher effectiveness training.

Hamilton, P.B. (1986). *An evaluation of a school discipline programme: 'Managing student behaviour: a whole school approach.'* Unpublished Masters dissertation. Murdoch University, WA.

Hargreaves, D. (1978) Deviance: The interactionist approach. In B. Gillham (Ed.) *Reconstructing educational psychology.* London: Croom Helm.

Johnson, N. (1985). *Teachers and implementing change.* Paper presented at the National Council of Education Centres, 4th National Conference, Hobart, Tasmania.

Kerr, D.M. (1984). *Changing schools to prevent delinquency.* Paper presented at the American Psychological Association Annual Convention, Toronto, Ontario, Canada.

Leach, D. (1981). *Innovating behaviour-based practices in schools.* Unpublished paper. School of Social Inquiry, Murdoch University

Sarason, S. (1971). *The culture of the school and the problem with change.* Boston: Allyn & Bacon.

Spirack, G.J., Platt, J.J. & Shure, M.B. (1976). *The problem-solving approach to adjustment.* London: Jossey-Bass.

Sulzer-Azaroff, B. & Mayer, G.R. (1977). *Applying behaviour analysis. Procedures with children and youth.* New York: Holt, Rinehart, Winston.

Thacker, V.J. (1982). *Steps to success: An interpersonal problem-solving approach for children.* Slough: NFER-Nelson.

Volumes 7, 8 and 9 (1990–92): Shortlisted papers

Educational psychologists as researchers: Some considerations for present and future practice
by Peter Gray, vol 8(1), 36–43.

Management of change by community groups
by Vanessa Parffrey, vol 8(2), 69–84.

Teachers, children and language difficulties in the primary school
by Jonathan Solity, vol 8(3), 16–31.

Helping children who are selectively mute
by Sylvia Baldwin & Tony Cline, vol 8(3), 72–83.

Panel Members
Convenor: Chris Shaldon, educational psychologist, Islington
Caoimhe Mcbay, educational psychologist, Islington
Andrea Dennison, educational psychologist, Dorset

Introduction by the panel

We were initially drawn to the title of our chosen paper as it highlighted both our own areas of interest as well as concerns that are very relevant to EP practice today – 'change', 'community' and 'groups'.

Parffrey is quite explicit from the outset that her intentions are to 'share' with the reader some 'stories' and that what validates this approach is the authenticity of 'being there' as opposed to reliance on theory and book knowledge. This is a challenging and refreshing opening. Parffrey is clearly championing the qualitative, narrative, pragmatic, experiential and reflective approach. Her intention is that 'through the sharing of experiences', there will emerge 'an exploration of our own role as psychologists, in participating in change'.

This paper does not however eschew all theoretical grounding. There is a clear underpinning of systems psychology to the analysis of the vignettes presented and a clear case is made for seeing relationships and reflection at the heart of systemic interaction. One of the most inspiring aspects of the paper is that it encourages us, as EPs, to apply such systemic thinking to our own working environment and to ourselves.

Equally encouraging is the range of potential work presented. The main body of the paper contains a description of four very different projects in which Parffrey was involved (a boys' grammar school ; a diocesan advisor to a vicar; a consultant to a housing association for young offenders; a youth counselling project). Such diversity is unusual but also very topical in relation to the current developments of children's services and the role of the educational/community psychology.

These four vignettes supply the real life interest of the paper. They reflect the complexity and fuzziness of action research. Only one of the four initiatives is deemed to be fully successful. The experience and reflection gained from the other three ventures, however, provides the basis for the wider learning shared at the end of the paper.

In the final section ('Issues arising'), Parffrey extracts common themes and issues that have emerged from the projects described. Again this is presented not in a dogmatic but in a questioning spirit. Identifying the belief systems, the underlying values and the common ethos within organisations is seen as a key factor for effective change.

Perhaps most importantly, the whole paper encourages the reader to reflect upon their own role as a psychologist when engaging in group or community or whole-school work. The spur to such reflection is provided by the shared stories, which connect with the reader on both an experiential and a reflective level.

In her conclusion, Parffrey writes of how educational psychology was seen to be at a 'time of flux and uncertainty' in 1991. She wrote that, 'because it is a time of change maybe, like the projects described here, there is no better time than now to be re-establishing just what we and our craft are about ?'

Seventeen years later this process of 're-establishment' is still as relevant, challenging and crucial as it was then.

Chris Shaldon, Andrea Dennison,
Caoimhe Mcbay

Address for correspondence
Chris Shaldon, 31A Maygrove Road,
London NW6 2EE
E-mail: Chris.Shaldon.camb-ed@
islington.gov.uk

Management of change by community groups

Vanessa Parffrey

In this paper, I should like to share with you others's stories – ones that I have been party to in a professional capacity – and to try to draw out a few common themes, i.e. the themes of groups wrestling with pressures, demands to change, new birth or reform.

Some organisational books will tell you what the problems are, and thus what I have to say might not be new in terms of content, but I have come to know them in a new way because I was there and the groups have come to solve some of these problems because they were there not because they had read books and theories on the subject.

What the paper will *not* be is a template of 10 easy ways to change community groups, but rather, through the sharing of others' experiences, it will lead us to an exploration of our own role, as psychologists, in participating in change. Factors which I hope will be interesting are the wide range of contexts in which the stories are set, the variety of models or structures used, and the similarity of process that emerges in the groups despite these variances. Some initiatives have a very clear structure, drawing mainly on a consultative way of working, while other projects take a more problem-solving approach, at least initially. But as we shall see not all projects end up quite the way intended!

I should say now that not all have been 'successful', although that word itself will emerge as one that needs further reflection. Not all have gone to plan or given rise to exactly what was hoped for; as I have said, this will not be a 'how to change community groups in 10 easy stages'. At best I can outline what we did, with whom and what some of the products were. The stages, if any, seem to have more to do with psycho-social development in the group, and therefore what it could achieve at any one time, than pre-arranged stages in the content. This idea of readiness within groups to take on and explore change, and their individualised response to that change, will emerge as an important variable in the projects as we describe them.

I take comfort from Ainscow's comments in his keynote address (1991) describing the process of change as messy and time-consuming, and Kerr's suggestion (1991) of a need to develop new concepts, processes and structures to facilitate change. Frederickson (Jones & Frederickson, 1990), too, ends her re-evaluation of systems work by suggesting that what we need is 'an approach that can handle the fuzziness and complexity of real-world problem situations'.

It would seem that handling change in real life is disorganised and far less amenable to prediction and control than we, as psychologists, would like to think. It seems to present a real challenge to a science of behaviour based on prediction and determinism. I make no apology, therefore, for presenting the stories in some qualitative detail in an attempt to do justice to what seems to be the messiness of individuals in organisations and the interpersonal and psychological issues that seem to block change.

For me, this seems to be what 'systems psychology' means – the psychology of individuals and groups of individuals within organisations and our relationship with them. I cannot help but feel that the term 'systems' has caused us to think of organisations and groups as entities and things rather than as collections of people with whom we, as psychologists, develop relationships. Perhaps this losing sight of the essentially psychological and interpersonal nature of systems work is why Checkland (1981) and Plas (1986) suggest that everyone talks of systems psychology but few seem actually to do it.

Here, then, is an offering. Its style and content is, I would think, what Frederickson (1990) would call 'soft systems' methodology, or Reason and Rowan (1981) 'new paradigm' research.

I am convinced that a reconceptualisation of systems psychology, along the lines that I have outlined above, will need the development of new modes of researching alongside groups in a more collaborative manner and so coming to know and share knowledge in quite different ways. I am, in this research, trying to remain true to this vision of collaboration and richness of detail in both its undertaking and its reporting.

It is for the reader to decide the validity and usefulness of this sort of approach in informing practice – the ultimate criterion of success in evaluating action research.

To provide a structure for describing the projects, I shall use Stufflebeam's CIPP framework of Context, Input, Process and Product (1971).

Project 1

Time allocation: 1 Baker day
10 x 1 weekly sessions
1 Baker day
Numbers: N = 60
EPs = 3 + 3 Trainees
C: A Grammar School
I: Intended input was the Western Australia package on Managing Student Behaviour involving all staff including four senior management team.

The first three sessions of the package were completed but it was clear that there were so many other, unconsidered issues blocking the task that the original programme was abandoned. Instead, the staff formed themselves into three self-selected working groups to look at communication, time and administration, and behaviour. Their brief was to come up with action plans and report back

to the whole staff at the next Baker day.

P: As below
P: 32 suggestions including the following which actually came to fruition: schools council, staff consultative committee, working parties on assessment. behaviour and homework (the last group included governors and parents) and a consultative exercise involving pupils looking at incentives and rewards.

Negotiation stage
The motives and needs of all those involved, e.g. head, patch psychologist and the team of psychologists, were high. There was an enormous commitment of time, money and staff and the expectations that such an investment could actually bring about change were equally high. Despite assurances to the contrary, I am not sure we ever really dispelled the myth of the hero-innovator.

The decision to undertake the course had, ostensibly, been taken by all the staff at the first Baker day. However, it is possible that there was some feeling that they 'ought' to say yes and therefore possibly a feeling of resentment at the time involved.

There was a disagreement as to whether the behaviour of the pupils was really so bad as to warrant such a high involvement from such a number of professionals. These matters not being clarified at the beginning, it is likely that the project began with each person hoping for quite different outcomes.

History
The history of the school and its past reputation as a highly academic school rested heavily on the staff's shoulders. The past headteacher's regime had been autocratic and dogmatic with a high level of patronisation and resultant dependency. The present skills and expectations of the staff therefore reflected this. The present head, for his part, was new and had 'come up through the ranks' of the present staff.

This past regime seemed also to affect the belief systems and attitudes within the school, i.e. there was clearly a sense of an external locus of control and a mistrust of any attempt to be consultative. This, in turn, affected the preparedness of the staff subgroups to take on responsibility and ownership of the initiative. It was as if they could not believe that they were genuinely being consulted or that they could have any effect on outcomes.

There also emerged a strong reaffirmation of their sense of individual autonomy as teachers and this rendered it difficult to foster a sense of community and corporate 'good'. They appeared 'selfish' and needy, evaluating any developments in terms of the effects on them rather than on the pupils. Interestingly, these same attitudes and beliefs were reflected in the boys' behaviour in, for instance, their schools council.

Ethos
The ethos of the school was not explicit - there was confusion over whether it really was working to a comprehensive ethic or whether it was still a grammar school with all that that meant in the town. Was it still a bastion of 'selective, exclusive masculinity'? Added to this (or indeed possibly exacerbating it) was the changing market place requiring more aggressive (masculine?) marketing. With this sort of culture in the school to work against, it might have been unwise of us to have used a process of model inset. Maybe we should have stuck with the more structured package model on the rationale of 'starting where your client is at'.

Renegotiation phase
Negotiating the change in direction of the crowd proved, during the evaluation, to be heavily resented by staff and SMT alike. They felt let down – as though we had moved the goalposts. This was despite the fact that, at the time, the SMT had been in full support.

In retrospect, it was clear that we, as a team, had repeated the error of the original negotiation, i.e. we had not consulted widely or thoroughly enough. We had made assumptions — we, too, had been patronising,

just like the management regime was perceived to be. As consultants, therefore, we had colluded with one of the most inhibiting features of the organisation.

The team of EPs
Due to the various and considerable demands on both the EPs' and the trainees' time, insufficient time was given by the team to form as a group themselves. There was not an opportunity to share our rationale, our motives, expectations, anxieties and beliefs. In a previous account of a similar project, the necessity of the team's having done something of this if service delivery is to change is illustrated. (Nichols et al., 1990)

I believe this project suffered from this crucial piece of business being neglected, and that the EPs apparently took on the particular dynamics of the organisation in that, for example, the issues of patronisation and responsibility were not solved. This illustrates the importance of some sort of external supervision or spiral consultancy.

Project 2
Time allocations: 1 year and 9 months
(9 x 1 monthly sessions)
1 Plenary
Numbers: N = 8
1 Consultant
C: Village suburb on edge of major city – working party appointed to look at five-year plan within the parish and how it might become more involved with the community. The leader of the parish, i.e. the vicar, was a member of the working party and his wife was the chair!
I: Philosophy aims and objectives structure
P: As described below
P: Short term: A two-year plan of ideas, projects, etc. with named people to take them on.
Long term:

Negotiation
A previous diocesan adviser had already worked with the team but in his words 'could not break the tyranny of the chair'. They had

clashed badly and publicly, and there had been little progress over a year. I then replaced him when he left the county. Incidentally, I was also called a diocesan adviser. This title seemed to be important regarding the authority structure of the group and its relationship with me.

It turned out that there were extremely high expectations that I would succeed where the previous person had not. Hitherto, the incumbent had experienced a good deal of criticism from key personnel within the parish and had also undertaken a full parish review with a team of four external consultants which had some difficult things to say about the parish and his style of management.

This history had, it seemed, led to a good deal of defensiveness on the part of the vicar and his wife. The wife protected her husband, which meant that any comment that could be interpreted as criticism was vehemently contested by her. He seemed very happy with this arrangement and remained a Pollyanna figure whenever problems were aired.

The group was made up of four women who seemed reluctant to voice their views, arguably because of the way any contrary viewpoints might be received; one professional man who wanted to run the sessions by task-oriented objectives; and another man who was new to the area and was reminded of that fact at every meeting.

Ethos

The ethos in this group had been discussed and clearly and explicitly written down. This, of course, for such a group was in terms of its commitment to the Church and the implications of that commitment in terms of reaching out to others in the community. A good deal of time was spent by the group articulating a very clear philosophy and ethos for the parish. In general, the structure worked – it provided a focus for our tasks and therefore a common purpose.

The statement of philosophy was very important in so far as it did bring people to-

gether both to share individualism and to develop some sort of corporatism. This part seemed to be relatively unthreatening to the leader and therefore went well. It also provided an essential bench-mark against which all other discussions and activities could be evaluated.

History

Again, like project 1, the history was of a paternalistic (but in fact matriarchal) pattern of leadership which had been in place for 20 years. The parish members were feeling ready for more individual responsibility and apparently were being urged to use it, but were not then actually given it.

It is interesting to reflect on the presence and extent of paternalism and maternalism within the Church generally and whether this was a specific manifestation of a more widespread pathology. Like the previous project, it was as if growth was being held back by history.

It is my belief, however, that through the opportunity to share and develop a common philosophy, and because the wife was in the chair, at least these dynamics were in some way public and could legitimately be confronted. This level of understanding and confrontation was never given an opportunity in the first project.

Attitudes and beliefs

Again, a belief or attitude seemed to be underlying the resistance to change in this group. It was something like 'you have got to do it my way – *the* way. No mistakes are allowed'. This resulted in no-one coming forward to help and widen the outreach of this particular group into the community for if they did, they were deemed unsuitable and asked to leave. This was not paranoia, it had actually happened. So there was a genuine fear of not fitting, of not being good enough and not being perfect enough. Other beliefs were as already mentioned, i.e. regarding criticism and how to cope with it. I wonder, too, as to the wife's belief in her husband's capacity to cope and deal with criticism for himself.

Despite these problems, I do believe that the leader, i.e. the vicar, was genuinely trying to give away power and balance direction and leadership with consultation, and that the chair was wrestling with that dynamic and trying to balance enthusiasm with patience. It seemed to me to be a group trying, on behalf of the wider organisation, truly to come to terms with its history in order that it could move forward.

By the end of this process many positive ideas had come forward; at a plenary meeting attended by some 200 people, they were supported by the whole parish. Priorities, timescales and named members to carry the process forward were identified and, at the time of writing, I understand many of these ideas have been implemented.

Even more importantly, several of the more inhibiting dynamics have been named, aired and done away wih. The vicar, for instance, says he feels more relaxed, supported and confident than he has in years. He also feels that he is doing his job better and is more willing to look at criticism constructively. This presumably frees his wife to channel her considerable energies into more creative activities than protecting him. Others in the group also remarked on how much more confident they felt about speaking up.

Interestingly, then, project 2 describes an organisation with some features potentially inhibiting change as in the first project, but one whose outcomes were much more 'owned' and total commitment much higher. There was also a feeling of having achieved something together as a parish, unlike the school where success was seen to be the result of a number of un-coordinated efforts made by a few.

Out of all the projects described, I see this one as the most 'successful' in terms of both outcome and process but not without the considerable cost of time and pain.

Project 3

Timescale:	5 months with a plan to have 10 sessions, 1 every 2 weeks.
Numbers:	N = 8 and 2 consultants

C: Housing association (inner-city) for young offenders. It was an ongoing project which had lost its way, i.e. had low occupancy rate, and was unclear of its future. The management committee had asked for a review; the project director had asked for such a review two years before.

The management committee was made up of multi-agency representation. This included a senior probation officer, the housing association representative, a senior social service representative, the project director and her deputy and three volunteer members who brought their own skills, for example, one was a sociology lecturer, one was a treasurer.

I: Philosophy, aims and objectives model used again. There were two consultants: one internal to the system – a probation officer – and one external, i.e. me.

P: Prolonged negotiation to clarify contract – of the purpose of the review, its membership, duration and dates. Ostensibly everybody wanted a review but everything seemed very long-winded and the group could not make decisions. The chair seemed reluctant to run the meetings and remained laid-back, literally, in terms of where he chose to sit and how he chose to take control, or not, of the meeting. The dates were continually left to the last minute of the meeting to arrange and then decisions about the dates of the review were put off because people were absent. The absentees from the group became very potent in the process of this group.

This group finally drew up an agreement as to the purpose of the review, etc., its conditions and its relationship with us as consultants. A date was arranged to start this process.

One working day before the meeting was due to start the chair phoned the co-consultant and after a long conversation about a whole manner of details and arrangements regarding the review the chair finally announced that he was resigning but that he intended to stick with the project until it had finished. This had not been his main purpose in ringing and he almost put it in at the last minute as an afterthought; he didn't see that it would necessarily affect any of the arrangements for the review.

We, as consultants, suggested that the resignation of the chair, albeit delayed for 10 weeks, meant that we should have a management meeting in order to discuss the implications of this resignation.

At that meeting there was a clear attempt to place responsibility for the review and this crisis meeting at our (the consultants) feet. The chair still could not see that his announcement had any effect on whether the review could continue; be seemed to deny any possibility of its having a more subtle effect on the messages that such a resignation gives to the project, to a review of that project and to the other participants.

There was still no acceptance of responsibility on his part and, again, a refusal, not just a reluctance, to chair it in terms of bringing together ideas, opening up a discussion, recording decisions and so on. The issue of a chair was then discussed at great length. Personal definitions of what a chair is were discussed and for approximately an hour and a half the group tried to decide therefore who would be the best person to take this role on. After an hour and a half there was still no decision and they decided therefore to have a rotating chair.

At this point the attention turned to dates and, again, there was extreme prevarication over those dates.

Consultant variables
One of us began to collude with the ownership and responsibility issue within the group and began to believe that we were responsible for organising and arranging, deciding about this review.

Another issue was about our own needs for this project to happen; my co-consultant wanted it professionally, especially as there were queries over the usefulness and future of his department, which was dedicated and committed only to doing consultancy and development work. I wanted this project to happen for my own research and indeed at this point had already committed myself to write this paper for this conference (the DECP annual course)! Therefore our needs were high and I think that this did add to a tendency for us to push the project slightly too fast.

Our own supervision suggested that we were becoming over-involved and that we should refer it all back to the management committee to decide whether they wanted a review and to approach us if and when they agreed to what they wanted. This created considerable anger with us and with the project director, presumably because she had wanted this review to happen for a very long time and had hoped that we two consultants could overcome the very real problems within the group. The other person who was angry was, predictably, the chair, presumably because we would not take on the role that he was supposed to be taking. It also ensued, and this is a very important point, that this chairperson was a Quaker and had very clear and definite ideas about leadership, about authority and about group behaviour, He believed passionately in democracy as a process that, given time, would always find its own solutions. This, for me, gave rise to very interesting reflections on the place of belief systems and group behaviour.

My own learning in this project was that I was more able to control my tendency to take over responsibility in a way that I had not done in the group in Project 1. This time I really was more able to stand still and not be sucked in and not to take on ownership. I did need to learn to take the risk of nothing happening and, perhaps in this case, my worst fears being confirmed.

This, however, causes some very real questions for educational psychologists: we, too, both within LEA and private work, have pressure on our jobs, we need to prove ourselves; the issue of being paid to do a job and therefore whether we can risk doing nothing; whether we can risk something we've been asked to do, not happening. Our needs as educational psychologists, our desires to get involved in projects with schools – do these override our skills as true enablers and consultants to these organisations?

This project also illustrated how important it is to clarify the purpose of an initiative that has been asked for – again this refers back to Project 1. It would seem that this is a very hard process but in itself will lead to some sort of clarity even if it is to realise that the group does not know or cannot agree and therefore maybe has to go in another direction or do some preliminary work for taking on the initiative it originally asked for.

This perhaps throws up the idea of readiness and that what an institution asks for is not always what they are ready to take on and another place of work might need to happen first. The risk for educational psychologists is that this other direction, this other place of work, may or may not involve the psychologist – again, this is difficult for both LEA and private psychologists who are wanting that work for their living.

Project 4

Timescale: 2 years
Numbers: N = 20

C: This was a new project, called 'The Torbay Youth Counselling Project'. It was a multi-agency initiative prompted by a Community Education Department directive from IDES re youth counselling services generally. I was involved initially as an LEA EP and then in an independent capacity.

I: No formal structure was implemented to launch this project.

P: Interestingly I was involved in the very initial stages of two such projects in two different towns, which have developed in quite different ways and with different speeds.

The initiative had arisen as a result of two different but complementary directives. The first was community education's response to the HMI report on youth counselling services which had concluded that counselling and advice to young people should be provided hand-in-hand. The other was the development in the town of the Children's Society project Startpoint, which had a brief to develop an information and advice service to young people in the area. Members of the steering group were drawn from the already existing inter-agency group in the town and so were well representative of every agency, both statutory and voluntary, and were well motivated to create some sort of counselling service for young people.

In the initial meetings there was much jostling over just whose baby this was going to be, i.e. who was going to fund it. The volunteer agencies were very keen to spend social services and education money but no agency, statutory or voluntary, was willing totally to underwrite it. (It was at this point in negotiations that a student EP on placement with me queried in his work diary what the psychological input was in this meeting and what the role of my presence could possibly be. I think this is an interesting question about what is psychology, what do psychologists do and what are appropriate roles for them, particularly when they are working in these rather broader community settings.)

The group was very large and rather formally chaired and the process was slow. This echoes the difficulties referred to in my paper on Tor Hill (Parffrey, 1990) regarding the difficulty of steering and having a direction when there are many agencies and therefore many positions and many philosophies involved. There was no attempt to reach a consensus on either the purpose or the nature of the project and no attempt was made to develop a plan to work to in order to steer this body forward. It was not always clear just who was chairing the meetings, the leadership seeming tentative and without direction. After many meetings an approach was made to various charities to sound out possible funding and therefore responsibility for this project. The NCH and the Children's Society were the two main charities that were approached regarding responsibility. This again echoes something of Projects 1 and 3 where no one person would take responsibility so they decided to look outside the group in the hope that something 'out there' would take on responsibility.

The final outcome of these negotiations with the charities was that the project would take place in this town and would receive joint Children's Society and Community Education money. An apparently cumbersome management structure was set up which gave full responsibility to the project leader of the Children's Society. This management structure was supported by the ongoing and original group of multi-agency representatives who formed a support group to carry on the planning and the impetus of the project.

This support group was, in fact, a volunteer group by this time, because their original roles and powers invested in them as representatives of their agency had now been superseded by the formation of this management group above them. However, it was this group that, a year later, appointed a co-ordinator for the project, who was seconded, by the education authority, to the Children's Society. This appointment was made very quickly for purposes of political expediency and future developments were hampered by the implications of this secondment not having been fully thought through. In particular, the line management of the co-ordinator and the different roles of the various groups were not clarified at this point.

However, there was high enthusiasm at this time about the project moving forward and very high and clear expectations (albeit false and unrealistic ones) that the ownership of this project was vested in the support group; in other words ownership and power was assumed by those who had not funded it. These assumptions and irrational beliefs did much, I would suggest, to compound difficulties for the co-ordinator but, again, due to the haste in which the appointment was made, went unchallenged.

As I say, at this point in the project, spirits were high but suddenly the project became entrapped. My interpretation of what then went on is in terms of parents who conceived the baby not letting it go to grow up and be independent. In particular, the project co-ordinator (newly appointed) was not allowed to have the freedom to run it his way. The support group became, in fact, an accountability group with the project co-ordinator having to report back and check out decisions and moves by the broader group. They wanted to know what was going on and they wanted to have a say and give advice to the co-ordinator regarding decisions. They expected their advice to be acted upon. They were unsure of their role and their power to control this growing infant. One of the questions might be, would their baby grow up as they had intended? Would she meet their needs to help adolescents? Would she further the values that they had brought to this project?

At this point, two of the original representative multi-agency group went independent in their own professional lives but remained involved as consultants to the project co-ordinator. This enabled me as one of those people to look afresh at the project and some of the dynamics that were entrapping it and holding it back from full development.

As consultants we suggested that the co-ordinator draw up a statement of the philosophy and aims of the project as a working document for the support group, to aid consensus-building and clarity of role. On reflection, the co-ordinator felt he was still meeting the support group's needs rather than his own and finally decided to:

1. write his own philosophy statement;
2. disband the support group – metaphorically cut the umbilical chord
3. using a group of four, develop a training and recruitment plan and to develop the philosophy doctrine and aims document into some sort of reality.

Again, the co-ordinator ran into difficulties

asserting his own needs rather than meeting the group's needs, even in this small group, and again needed time to withdraw and reflect.

This process from the beginning of looking at philosophy and aims as a way forward through to his second retreat into personal reflection took five months. Twelve volunteer workers for the counselling project have now been selected and are halfway through their training; they are due to start delivering the counselling service this month.

P: The co-ordinator has now developed a new supportive relationship with his opposite number in another town and seems freer to use other people as and when appropriate.

It is as if he has finally managed to solve the problems of attachment and separation that, to me, seem to pervade this particular project. Is it not pertinent that the project itself is about adolescent needs and the establishment of independence, separation and individual identity?

The experience of this project for me was very similar to my Torhill experience, as referred to before, of the difficulty of working with multi-agency groups. It seems to be particularly important to clarify philosophy and purpose of any project at the beginning, which then helps to clarify roles and increase commitment to the project. It also helps clarify the symmetry of relationships and the authority and leadership style appropriate to the project.

It also raises the issue of working with volunteers or those giving up time from other employment. Just how much time can be asked of people and, if they do, just what is in it for them? Moreover, should the paid officer be concerned about these issues? Whose responsibility is it to manage volunteers? These burning issues, perhaps unnoticed in mainstream educational psychology, are of paramount importance when working with community groups.

Issues arising

I could go on describing other ventures: Torhill, the IT scheme I've already mentioned, other schools and parishes and groups that I have worked with. I am in the process of collecting more qualitative, questionnaire and interview data from 30 parishes regarding their experiences of change initiatives.

So what are some of the lessons learnt and common issues arising?

In most areas, I have tried to explore the issues that seem to have emerged in the form of questions that might prove useful to reflect on when involved in a change initiative.

1. Negotiation phase
a) Just what is everyone expecting in terms of *outcome* and respective *roles*?
   Issues of mutual expectations about the initiative need to be shared at this point but the difficulties of really clarifying them seem fraught with difficulty, not least because of the uncertainty of what might emerge in the course of the project.
   Attitudes to changing direction and plans, if necessary, might fruitfully be explored at this point – i.e. can/should the contract be 'good enough'?

b) Why is the group asking *you*, and why *now*? What is it they are hoping you will be? Hero-innovator? Guru? How does this make you feel? Are you prepared to receive anger or to be disappointed or to be unpopular? Do you really want to give away psychology and power? Especially when psychological services are under threat?

c) Why are *you* doing it? Is it to assert yourself, your values and your service? Are any of these under threat? Just what is the level of investment in this project personally and as a team? Do you want it too much? Can the project possibly repay such hopes and expectations?

d) What is the 'point of pain' within the group or organisation? What is the *raison d'être* for change? Is it coming from without or within? Is it strong enough to provide the perseverance and motivation when the going gets rough?

2. History and tradition

a) What is the group's experience of leadership styles? Of consultation and consultants (or psychologists)? Of past changes? Have these experiences been of autocracy and patronage? Have they been happy or painful?

b) What is the *reputation* of the organisation? If high or well-known, what are the implications for considering change? Anxieties over losing customers – 'they might not like me any more if I change' – are very real and will need attention.

c) What is their experience of you?

d) What actually is the organisation or group *for*? If it is about caring for people and looking after them, as often charitable, religious or service organisations are, then how does this ethic inhibit the development of a more symmetrical, collaborative relationship? This last point is linked both with the next, but also with the peculiar nature of working with community groups (see no. 7 below). Personally, I think this a pivotal issue in the development of collaborative styles within public services, including psychological services.

3. Belief systems

What are the predominant beliefs within the organisation, e.g. regarding locus of control and power, definitions of leadership, self-esteem, attitudes to making mistakes or taking risks? Is there a mismatch between individual definitions and meanings and, say, management's?

4. Readiness

There certainly seems to be a concept of readiness linked with organisational maturity and independence. Whereas some groups take off with their ideas and develop them after very short inputs or projects, other take several years to show any evidence of moving. The latter are often those schools, parishes, families or groups that seem to call in every available resource one after the other (usually without telling one resource about the other) and yet still remain quite determined not to change. The members of the group seem united in their common task – to resist change – and this they do most successfully!

It would seem, then, that sometimes we are asked in to do a particular piece of work with a group or organisation but that often there is other work that the group needs to do first. This may or may not involve us as psychologists and, again, our willingness to let go of the initiative even when needs to continue are high, is crucial.

Just what it is that allows some groups really take off is, for me at least, still a mystery. Some of the leaders of the projects described here talk of the right personnel in place at the right time. But my sense of enquiry pushes me to want to know more – it is a notion still requiring much more work.

5. Small group versus large group

This heading is purposely ambiguous – there seems to be the dilemma over whether to work with a small, mandated sub-group of the larger group or whether to work only with the large group but there are also the apparent difficulties, even rivalries, which emerge between sub-groups and between a sub-group and the large group.

Such difficulties and inter-group rivalries are avoided if only the large group is worked with but reaching consensus, developing identity and all the other prerequisites of group effectiveness, are, of course, made extremely slow in large groups.

Certainly, in this research, where the small group was genuinely consultatively mandated by the larger organisation, progress was both rapid and 'owned' by the large group. Where the entire staff of a school was involved, however, the sub-groups formed to make working parties took on a life of their own and tended to do their own thing. It proved difficult to hold on to a sense of contributing to something bigger than just the small group and its close boundaries.

Interestingly, it has transpired that the school which undertook an initiative with a small representative group (and with spectacular results) was envious of another school where the entire staff were involved but with less obvious results. It would seem that possibly working only with the wider group there is the chance of a higher yield but with much higher risk of failure. Working with change increasingly makes one feel more like a risk evaluator than a psychologist!

6. Psychologist/consultant variables

The issues here are about whether to work as an individual, as a pair or as a team and the different resources and supervision implications. The stories illustrated an example of each of these modes of working.

a) The danger of collusion in the psychology of the organisation. 'Spiral consultancy' (Brown & Burden, 1987) certainly has emerged as being essential.

b) The need to give *time* for the team or pair of psychologists to develop a shared understanding of philosophy and practice. (see also Nichols et al., 1989).

c) The use of one consultant 'external' to the system and one 'internal' seems to be emerging as a useful balance. This may be the use of the patch psychologist with another member of the county team, say, or, like the example described above, could be an in-house consultant with a bought-in one from a totally different background.

d) The consultant must have credibility within the system as regards competence, knowledge and trust. In the above model, the in-house worker gives vicarious credibility to the outsider.

e) Whether the consultant must also have authority and clout within the system is a parameter still being explored. In some

of the initiatives currently being evaluated, it has been the bishop who has acted as consultant. This is equivalent to the CEO undertaking a project with a school. Whether this is a serious hindrance to change or, in fact, an encourager is yet to be discovered.

7. Particular problems of multi-agency work and/or involvement of volunteers

Exploring change with *community* groups has, I think, particularly highlighted these rather specific difficulties. Where there are several stakeholders in a project, whether financial or emotional, it would seem to increase the complexity considerably (see also Parffrey, 1990). I interpret this as the difficulty in reaching a corporate consensus of purpose and methodology; different agencies bring a different 'model of man' and thus will have different aims, different methods to achieve their ends and different agendas.

Add to this the very often ambivalent attitude towards and treatment of the voluntary agencies – a sort of 'we'll have your time and use your commitment but don't expect to have a say in anything really important' attitude – and you have a situation which is very complex indeed with often a whole variety of hidden agendas of both a political and emotional nature.

These particular problems bring me to my final and, to me the most important, 'lesson learnt'.

8. Developing a common ethos or philosophy

The opportunity to develop a common philosophy and common purpose seems to me to be crucial. Not just, I believe, because it conforms to the problem-solving process which is to clarify the problem before you can find a solution.

Rather it is, I would suggest, because it allows for an open debate, an acknowledgement of the underlying values and belief systems inherent in the system in the organisation. It would be common place *à la* Maslow to speak of individual and basic needs requiring attention before more corporate or higher order issues can be looked at, but putting these last two points together, maybe it is values, therefore, that form a very basic need in humankind.

In the examples I have given where the group did have a chance to explore these fundamental values and where there was therefore an opportunity to reach some sort of common consensus, a good-enough agreement, then the project seemed to take some shape and have some vector and arguably had more impetus to overcome some of the very real problems of interpersonal dynamics. Where we didn't do that, i.e. Project 1 and, at first, Project 4, it seemed that the project ran into confusion and lost direction.

I also believe that identifying a common ethos also allows for the development of a sense of community to which members can belong. Once this has been established, so a common purpose and relevant tasks and roles can be identified. This in turn increases commitment and a sense of being valued and of contributing. These are, of course, only hypotheses generated by the research so far but it is with these ideas that I will be enquiring with future groups.

I think this has a crucial message for educational psychologists and psychology in general; in the States and in Britain the organisational development movement, I believe, has ignored it to their peril, and quantitatative management by objective models of OD is limited. I think there is some evidence in the United States literature that they too have hit a brick wall by only using a problem-solving, more mechanistic approach – again we might be back to Frederickson, the hard-system approach.

The issue of developing a common purpose and underlying philosophy poses us as educational psychologists a very pertinent question. Are we, indeed, clear what our mission ethos or value position is – particularly at a time of flux and uncertainty? Indeed, arguably, *because* it is a time of change maybe, like the projects described here, there is no better time than now to be re-establishing just what we and our craft are about?

Another issue that emerges for me personally, and this is linked with the one I've just been talking about, is what I have learnt while doing this work. I have been confronted with my own attitude to change and been caused to question just why I have come to be working in this way with these groups at this lime.

It seems to be something about my belief systems and my values that cause me to work in this particular way with these particular people. Amongst it, there are losses, there are risks; there are ambivalences and confusion; there is plenty of opportunity for confrontation of my own attitudes and Achilles' heels. There is also joy and fun and a sense of having moved (although I am not always quite sure where!).

Certainly I have come full circle, moving from an individual psychology of organisations through to groups and to what I would call systems psychology, but by reflecting on what that means and by challenging both the facts of organisations and colleagues who are also working in this area, I think I have come back to seeing that at the heart of systemic interaction are indeed our selves, and our selves in relation to individuals, groups and that organisation.

I end, therefore, with a quote from Fox, Pratt and Roberts' article in *Educational Psychology and Practice*, November 1990, where they are talking about psychologists' work in secondary schools, a process model for change, and I quote:

> *Educational psychologists need to see a change in their own activities as a starting point for any change in school. Therefore educational psychologists need to overcome their own resistance to change if they are to model for a school the possibility of effective change.*

Dave Kearney (1989) too, reminds us of the need to re-examine our professional belief systems particularly at a time of rapid change. And so we come full circle. Exploring the management of change within community groups prompts us to reflect on our own management of change. In the proceedings of the 1989 DECP course *Asserting Psychology in the Market Place* (Hornby and Parffrey, 1989) our editorial ended with this challenge: National initiatives are challenging psychology and psychologists to grasp the nettle of its own revolution and change.

Are we ready to grasp it and so allow psychology to take its rightful place in the community?

Two years on – at this year's course called *A Psychology for the Community* – I find myself asking the same question.

References

Ainscow, M. (1991), Effective schools for all: An alternative approach to special needs in education *(this volume)*.

Brown, E. & Burden, R. (1987) Educational psychologists as agents of school organizational development. *Educational Change and Development, 1.*

Cockman, P. (1981). Systems thinking, systems practice. Chichester: Wiley.

Fox, M., Pratt, P. & Roberts, S. (1990). Developing the educational psychologist's work in secondary schools: A process model for change. *Educational Psychology in Practice, 6*(3), 163–169.

Hornby, T.-A. & Parffrey, V. (1989). Asserting psychology in the market place II. *Educational and Child Psychology, 6*(4).

Jones, N. & Frederickson, N. (1990). *Refocusing educational psychology.* Lewes: Falmer Press.

Kearney, D. (1989). Examining professional belief systems. *Educational and Child Psychology, 6*(4).

Kerr, A. (1991). Leadership and our community *(this volume)*.

Nichols, L., Parffrey, V. & Burden, R. (1989). Preventing disruptive behaviour in schools. *School Psychology International,* 10(4).

Parffrey, V. (1990) *An alternative to exclusion: Tor Hill.* Educational Psychology in Practice, 5(4), 216–221.

Pleas, J. (1986). *Systems psychology in the school.* Oxford: Pergamon Press.

Reason, P. & Rowan, J. (1981). *Human inquiry.* Chichester: Wiley

Stufflebeam, D. (1971). *Educational evaluation and decision-making.* Peacock Publishers: Itasca, IL.

Volumes 10, 11 and 12 (1993–95): Shortlisted papers

Educational psychology: What future?
by Tony Dessent, vol 11(3), 50–54.

Applying the ideas of quality assurance to an educational psychology service: A good idea but does it apply to me?
by Irvine Gersch & David Townley, vol 11(3), 55–61.

A consultation approach to the educational psychologist's work with schools
by Patsy Wagner, vol 12(3), 22–28.

Solution-focused brief therapy, educational psychologists and schools
by Yasmin Ajmal & John Rhodes, vol 12(4), 16–21.

Panel Members
Convenor: Anne Powell-Davies, senior educational psychologist, Telford and Wrekin
Carole Jones, educational psychologist, Derby City
John Franey, programme director (initial EP training), University of Bristol

Introduction by the panel

For its contemporary relevance, its 'quick history' that outlines context, suggested explanation for where and how the profession was positioned in 1994, and pertinent predictions for PEP and service placement and restructuring, colleagues unanimously selected Dessent's (although written from his conference presentation by Indoe and Lunt) prophetically titled article, *What Future?*

A few words initially to commend the reader to revisit the remaining three papers on our reading list:

- Ajmal & Rhodes' consider how they used learning theory to introduce and embed solution focused brief therapy (SFBT) into their service practice. The piece applies principles of planning, reflection, and explores the role of new knowledge creation within organisations. In advocating 'do-ability', they suggest 'using the same time differently', and promote empowerment and collaborative working through SFBT and consultation.

- Wagner shares her 'practical and robust model of work for the practising educational psychologist'. Consultation is now widespread, while its use remains broad and varied. This preventative approach 'puts collaboration at the centre of the activities of the educational psychologist'. Wagner looks at why consultation may be the answer to the challenges of a within-child approach fostered by 1981 Act, and highlights the underlying psychology, and therefore the distinctive contribution of the EP.

- Gersch and Townley urge us to consider quality assurance, exploring parallels and possibilities of models in business and commerce, Total Quality Management (TQM) and the opportunities and challenges of applying such models to the management of educational psychology services. Contemporary issues such as the tension between consistent and recognisable service delivery and professional autonomy are explored, and these remain very relevant issues.

And so to Dessent. He offers us a concise analysis of the challenges facing the profession in 1994 and these remain strikingly pertinent to 2008. He explores a recipe for a new 'service' culture, with basic ingredients including delegation, consultation, marketing and partnership. Many areas still hold true for the profession, the recognition that there will never be enough resources, therefore understanding the need to prioritise and target in as consistent and transparent way as possible. Indoe and Lunt's write-up does not touch upon our role of researcher, or that of encouraging action research to be undertaken in partnership with fellow professionals in schools, the local authority and children and young people. Was this so far from our thoughts in the early 1990's?

To demonstrate there is more to our work than professional 'definer' we continue to need to discover ways of raising the profile of the profession and being explicit about the skills of EPs, the range of knowledge and the opportunities to apply psychology. There may never be a better opportunity to demonstrate these aspects. Having just completed a day of interviews to appoint a trainee EP to our service, we have been excited by the calibre of applicants, their positive expectations of the role and the confidence of their psychology. If Dessent was holding up a mirror in 1994, what can reflections today offer us in respect of taking a confident professional step into our preferred future?

Anne Powell Davies, Carole Jones, John Franey

Address for correspondence
Anne Powell-Davies, Senior Educational Psychologist & Telford Team Leader, Glebe Centre, Wellington TF1 1JP. E-mail: Anne.Powell-Davies@telford.gov.uk

Educational psychology: What future?

Tony Dessent

This write-up was produced by Derek Indoe and Ingrid Lunt from notes taken at the talk and checked by the author.

I T WOULD BE very foolish to lay down a set of rules about what educational psychologists should do in the present context of changing legislation; nor am I speaking on behalf of the educational psychology service in Nottinghamshire – their own principal is quite able to represent their views.

What educational psychologists do is determined by the requirements and the context of their work. Few educational psychologists are hero innovators (which is probably a good thing because hero innovators only last a short time).

Let me begin by trying to describe the context in which I work. My employer is Nottinghamshire County Council. The section (Pupil and Community Services) I head includes the educational psychology service as well as services dealing with section 11, educational welfare, special education, the under fives, crime prevention, drug prevention, and liaison with health, social service departments, and the police. Special education is the largest section of Pupil and Community Services and has the largest budget. Nottinghamshire used to have a large number of pupils educated in special schools though this is fast reducing with a 36 per cent reduction in special school enrolments over the past three years and with proposals to close a number of special schools next year.

One can describe the culture of Nottinghamshire as having a high profile Education Committee. The 'Committee' likes to have a policy and a say on most aspects of education. You might say Nottinghamshire is proud, cerebral and buoyant. Education in Nottinghamshire is seen as a good thing and has a high profile.

However, there have been recent changes in the culture. Delegation (which is moving rapidly), business plans and marketing, internal trading, consultation and partnership are all relatively new ingredients. In Nottinghamshire as in most LEAs the *schools perspective* is the focus of the moment with a shift from what has been described as the 'command culture' to 'service culture'.

A quick history of special needs, and educational psychologists' roles

English educational history as it bears upon special needs has a predictable circularity. We begin with payment by results which goes back as far as 1870 when some children were seen as being unable to meet the standards set by the school board. Those of you who remember Form 2 HP know that it involved a report on a child who was examined for a disability of mind. From labels such as 'mental defective' we moved to 'ascertainment' and 'categories of handicap' and 'educational subnormality'. Circular 2/75 first talked of 'special educational treatment' and 'SE' forms. Next came Warnock in 1978 leading to 'statements of special educational need'. These were followed by the 1988 Act with 'exemptions' and 'disapplications'. One could make many comparisons between the 1993 Act and the 1870 Act.

Throughout all this legislation there is a circularity of certain dimensions: i.e. localisation/centralisation, integration/segregation, generalists/specialists. The pendulum swings back and forth across history. The one constancy you can depend upon is that a system has always required formal statutory procedures and associated paperwork for separating out some children in some way.

A key role of the educational psychologist in all of this is separating out, and defining the 'specialness', or 'resourceworthiness' of some children. Our education system requires someone to define 'specialness', or 'to find the two per cent'. It will always need someone to do this as their central function. The work of an educational psychologist is linked to the requirements of the special education system. However, EPs have rarely been comfortable in confronting this fact of life viz that their purpose is largely to serve social, political and economic functions.

Instead EPs have historically construed their roles in the following ways:

- 'treat' the child (e.g. using therapy, psychometrics and diagnosis);
- 'treat' the teacher (e.g. using INSET, PAD, other packages in the 'cargo culture', behavioural methods);
- 'treat' the parents (e.g. using portage or paired reading);
- 'treat' the LEA/sort out the school system (e.g. using systems work, or adopting an advisory role re policy).

Secondly, the need for the EP is based upon the fact that there is no agreement about what are special educational needs. The existence of educational psychologists is dependent on everyone's inability to define special educational needs. This produces a need for a professional 'definer'. Thirdly, the EP's existence is required because meeting special educational needs is about attitudes and values and positive discrimination. To function effectively and efficiently the system needs 'resource definers' both to ensure protection and positive discrimination for the most vulnerable but also, paradoxically, to limit positive discrimination to the assessed few.

Three areas relevant to EPS quality and the survival of educational psychologists

i) Some enduring characteristics of policy and provision for children with special educational needs
There will never be enough resources. There will always be unmet needs. The system requires a means of targeting priorities.

To manage the system there is a need for a unit of management larger than a school and smaller than the Department for Education. There will always be tensions between the competing needs of pupil groups (e.g. 'the other pupils', 'the gifted', 'the dyslexic'). There will always be tensions between stakeholders such as LEAs, schools, parents and voluntary groups. There will always be pressures as well as ethical and moral dilemmas and choices enmeshed by mythology and anecdotal evidence.

The system will always need someone to blame.

ii) The 1990s – some new facts of life
In the 1990s demands for the following will increase:

    accountability
    public scrutiny
    transparency
    reducing the secret garden
    objectivity
    moderation
    corporate decision making
    local control
    consumerism/choice
    consistency
    minimum standards
    central guidelines
    cost effectiveness
    value for money
    devolution/delegation
    concern about monitoring

iii) Local education authorities -their future roles
These are the likely roles of the local authority in the future.

- As moral leader
    - giving direction in social and political priorities
    - seeking maximum collaboration/ consensus
    - protecting minority interests and ensuring equal opportunities
    - monitoring the implications of delegation
- As planner
    - acting as a unit of management
    - looking to low prevalence needs

- of specialist services and provision
- taking the role of co-ordinating services
- As the definer of resource allocations
  - using formulae/carrying out audit
  - ensuring the consistency of statementing
  - setting up moderating groups

Potential roles for educational psychology services arising from these areas might be:
- Defining role 'business as usual'
- Negotiation role – achieving maximum consensus with stakeholders on devolved resources
- Monitoring/accountability
- Regulator
  – ensuring equity/consistency
- Advocacy -for child and parent
  – for schools
- Handling trouble
- Training – major generic adviser to LEA

The 1990s – some personal predictions
- the restructuring of services
- the restrucuring of principal educational psychology posts
- the integration of educational psychology services in broader education service structures
- the importance of the LEA special needs policy in shaping the educational psychologist's role
- the importance of the LEA political context
- corporate developments across the council departments
- parental pressure – appeals
- pressure to define the aspects of the educational psychology service that can be delegated

Service assets and deficits
a) The assets
Within a changing context it is worthwhile to look at your strengths as well as weaknesses, opportunities and threats. If we look at the assets educational psychology services have to ensure their quality and survival they are many:

- The statutory requirement for educational psychology services (will this be forever?)
- The ability to connect individual needs to systems for meeting needs
- The 'eyes and ears of the LEA'
- Objectivity, impartiality and breadth of assessment (generic SEN role)
- The ability to recognise relativity/exceptionality of needs
- The ability to observe and use a wide range of diverse solutions to problems in different contexts
- The professional educational voice in a multidisciplinary world of special educational needs

b) The deficits
Conversely there are many factors that militate against the survival and quality of psychological services.
- A continuing confusion about who is the customer
- The need to resolve 'service' versus 'autonomous professional' conflict
- An inconsistency of practices within and between services
- The wide variation in theoretical and conceptual frameworks
- The variable linkage of services to LEA policy
- The variable co-ordination of psychological and other local authority services
- Unrealistic expectations by clients
- The 'iceberg syndrome' (I was once shadowed for a week by a senior special needs official from the Department for Education who at the end of the week announced her surprise that no 'dyslexics' had been discovered. Her job with the DfE, which was dominated by dyslexia, only saw the tip of the SEN iceberg.)

What part of the iceberg does your Chief Education Officer see, do psychologists make him/her see?

Conclusion – directions for the future

The LEA is the main customer for educational psychology services. Hence the need to define the service role and target service delivery primarily to the LEA. To many services this will be business as usual. However, as a core part of the LEA, educational psychology services need to avoid self-protecting strategies and to focus upon improving normally available provision for children with special needs rather than perpetuating statutory assessments as a means of delivering resources. As devolution proceeds EPs will need to assist LEAs in maximising the safe delegation of special educational needs resources to schools. There is scope to develop a negotiation role to achieve maximum consensus with stakeholders in line with the LEA's moral leadership role. The LEA still has a planning role. Educational psychologists are well placed to act as major generic advisers, to perform a monitoring/evaluation role. They should seek to provide the highest level of cross service professional consistency within a broad church. Services should be prepared to be transparent in their work, and demonstrate accountability. They will also need to improve awareness of what they do, demonstrate their cost effectiveness and articulate how the educational psychology service enables the local authority to provide cost effectively for children with special needs.

Volumes 13, 14 and 15 (1996–98): Shortlisted papers

Learning to learn, phenomenography and children's learning
by Chris Walker, vol 15(3), 25–33.

Reading development and its difficulties
by Margaret Snowling with a reply by Rea Reason, vol 15(2), 44–68.

The bunny bag: A dynamic approach to the assessment of preschool children
by Judy Waters and Phil Stringer, vol 14(4), 33–45.

What would happen if? Personal construct psychology and psychological intervention
by Tom Ravenette, vol 13(4), 13–20.

Panel Members
Convenor: Philip Prior, principal educational psychologist, Wandsworth
Christine Devonshire, educational psychologist, Leicester City
Heather Northcote, educational psychologist, Derbyshire

Introduction by the panel

All four articles that we considered had a great deal to recommend them. And, as one would hope, apart from their intrinsic qualities, each illuminated in their own way what a broad church applied educational psychology has become both as a profession and as an academic discipline. However, even more than this they show how applied educational psychology has such potential to become a creative force in the way we understand and engage with the lives of the children and young people we work with.

The article by Maggie Snowling is rooted in rigorous empirical research and encapsulates the links between our developing understanding of neuroscience, models of learning and cognition, and the practical issues relating to why some children have such difficulty learning to read. Judy Waters and Phil Stringer highlight the (then) challenges concerning developing the practice of dynamic assessment, which was still perceived by many as a rather esoteric and singular form of assessment. Through the development of the Bunny Bag, Judy surely helped to broaden the applicability and use of dynamic assessment in Britain. The third article, by Chris Walker, speculates, via the prism of a drama lesson conducted by Dorothy Heathcote, how children learn, describe and understand the process of their own learning and their existential interaction with the world around them. Chris presents this from a phenomenological perspective, and the journey she describes in developing such understanding had strong links with the article by Tom Ravenette that we finally chose.

Following in the footsteps of George Kelly, Tom began practicing, developing and writing about the application of Personal Construct Theory in the 1960s. The 60s and 70s was an extraordinarily creative period in terms of the development of groundbreaking and innovative uses of psychology, coupled with radical re-interpretations of concepts of mental health (and mental illness). Throughout this period Tom extended the language of PCP as it applied to the work of EPs, writing papers such as *Psychologists, teachers, children: how many ways to understand?* (1972); *To tell a story, to invent a character, to make a difference* (1979); and *Never, never, never give advice* (1980; for all references, see Ravenette, 1997). Whilst not all EPs will refer to 'bi-polar' constructs in their everyday work, arguably the practice of every one us in some way or other will have been influenced by Tom's work. But for many, Tom rightly remains an outstanding figure within the profession and the article you are about to (re)read contains many of the inspirational motifs that can be found in all his work. In the article, Tom does so much more than merely describe a technique or method, but attempts to articulate ('as seen through half closed eyes') some essential truths about what we are about as psychologists, our relationships with 'clients' and those who work with them, and the importance of the way in which we dynamically engage with all the situations and contexts in which we might find ourselves. At its heart lies a powerful understanding of the primacy and importance of emotional engagement with those with whom we work and as the fundamental force upon which the success of so many interventions hang.

Tom, through PCP, also anticipated many of the developments that have since become part of the topography of modern applied educational psychology, such as client-centred and solution-focused approaches (a scaling question is nothing if not a bi-polar construct); story telling; narrative approaches; appreciative enquiry; and consultation in all its forms. In addition a creative, reflective, questioning approach and above all else, a sense of humility about our place in the greater scheme of things, such as his description of his anticipation of a meeting about James, the young man around who this article revolves:

A meeting of this nature is always an adventure in the sense that one never knows what will happen. It is also a challenge to one's professional core constructs – can I cope? Can I make sense of things? Can I intervene to make a difference? My basic tool is the question...'

Philip Prior, Christine Devonshire, Heather Northcote

Address for correspondence
Philip Prior, Wandsworth EPS, The Town Hall, Wandsworth High Street, London SW18 2PU
E-mail: PPrior@wandsworth.gov.uk

Reference
Ravenette. A.T. (1997). *Tom Ravenette: Selected papers. Personal construct psychology and the practice of an educational psychologist.* Farnborough: EPCA Publications.

What would happen if? Personal construct psychology and psychological intervention

Tom Ravenette

THE FOCUS of this paper is psychological intervention using a personal construct framework in relation to children who present problems to teachers, care staff and others. Although the work itself is currently carried out in a residential setting for 'disturbed' or 'disturbing' children, it represents something of my own continuing development both in practice and in theory from work in a school psychological service. The sequence I propose to follow is to tell the first part of a story, then to present Personal Construct Theory 'as seen through half closed eyes' abstracting just two of its themes which will then be seen to be central in the resumed narration of my story. The themes in question are 'Alternative constructions', which stems from the theory's underlying philosophical stance, and 'Contrasts', a broadening of the notion of bi-polar constructs (see below). I shall conclude by making some observations about PCP and the development of imagination in psychological intervention.

The story

I was asked to meet the care staff in one of the houses of a residential school to discuss James, now 15 years old, whose behaviour was a serious concern. It had been planned for me to interview James but because of his behaviour at the weekend he had been sent home and had not yet returned. It so happened that I had interviewed James about a year before. At that time he had attended the school on site but had proved too bright and was admitted to a mainstream school which at that date did not see him as a problem. This report was available and from it I quote the

first two and last two paragraphs. As will be seen they say something both of his history and of my observations on the interview itself.

James has only been at this residential school for a short time and presents something of a conundrum. He has a long chequered history of disturbing behaviour, different schools and different agencies. None of this is apparent here. The one thing that is generally acknowledged is that he is intelligent. An important aspect of his upbringing is a history of splits in the family, rejection by his mother almost from birth, living with a stepmother who did not like him, moving to live with father and a succession of his girlfriends, further rejections.

Throughout the interview it was my impression that although he responded to my questions it was as though he was psychologically absent but physically present. This was particularly the case when I attempted to go beyond his superficial answers. A full record of the interview would be utterly confusing since the content of his responses effectively defined the context as one of not going beyond the obvious. This, then, implicitly led to his 'self-definition' as intelligent and co-operative but … And his definition of me as someone he could string along with pat answers whilst giving away nothing personal.

The final paragraphs read:
I brought the interview to an end by reminiscing about a farmer sowing his seed in the winter and at first seeing nothing ('of course' said James). Come the spring he

looked out and saw sprouts of green coming through the soil. Perhaps some of my questions might be like the farmer's seed and just a few only might sprout.

I then told him that the interview was finished and that he could go back to his class. He was completely taken aback and did not know how to respond. Somewhat hesitatingly he walked across to the door and left. If I am right that the interview was fundamentally about interactions rather than content it is just possible that he saw it as an event in which his constructions of me and his presentation of his 'sense of self' would receive confirmation. In reality I suspect that I invalidated both and consequently he was thrown.

Personal Construct Psychology through half closed eyes

At school, when the art lesson was 'object drawing', the teacher gave a very useful suggestion. 'Look at the object with half closed eyes,' he would say, 'then you will see the essential form.' Confronted with the task of presenting something of a Personal Construct Psychology as simply as possible at various workshops I was reminded of that advice and what follows is my own version, conceding, of course, that others might produce a different account.

(1) Individuals create their own personal meanings of themselves and their worlds

(2) out of their awareness, at different levels of consciousness and with affective, cognitive and conative aspects, of

(3) similarities and differences

(4) arising from the succession of events with which they are confronted.

(5) these discriminations lead to the development of two-ended, i.e. bi-polar, constructs

(6) which then become inter-related into various systems

(7) enabling individuals to anticipate, with varying degrees of success,

(8) the likely outcomes of their encounters with the world.

(9) Central to these systems are core constructs whereby individuals define themselves

(10) and these are essential for the maintenance of a 'sense of self'.

(11) Persons' behaviour at any moment stems from their constructions of themselves and their circumstances at that time and

(12) they choose that alternative which seems most apt.

(13) the theory is underpinned by the principle of constructive alternativism, i.e. that there never is an inevitably 'right' view of things, but rather there will always be alternatives, some of which may well not as yet exist.

Some of these statements are already exemplified in the report on James which I have given above. For example, the bi-polar construct describing him as 'psychologically absent – physically present' (5); my inferences as to his 'self-definition' (9); together with his implied definition of me (1); and reference to the interview confirming or invalidating his expectations (8).

Psychological intervention

Problems
We become involved when a teacher, or care worker, makes a referral, i.e. an implicit request for help. When this happens we need to recognise that there is never just one problem. The fact of referral already reflects the likelihood that either the worker's sense of competence in coping or skill in understanding – each of which is probably a core construct at a professional or personal level – is at stake. This will seldom be stated as such, but when pressed the referrer may acknowledge it. The usual complaint will be about a child, often with the assertion that he or she has problems, or special needs, whereas in reality it is the child's behaviour or failures which are problematic for the referrer. Not infrequently the child will deny having problems but instead will make complaints about

what the world does to him or her. In either case, referrer or child, there will be invalidations in their respective ways of making sense of the world together with threats to their 'sense of self'. As I see things it is the implicit awareness that core constructs are at risk which creates problems, although failures in understanding as such may certainly lead to difficulties.

I was led to this view by the story of Miss B. She had referred a boy ostensibly for his failing to learn to read. I could find nothing in my interview with him which might help to understand the situation but noted his attitude of 'keep away, hands off'. I discussed this with the teacher but felt completely at a loss as to how I might make a difference. In despair I took my courage in both hands and asked how, deep down, she saw herself. After a long pause she commented on the difficulty of my question and then said 'I suppose it is that I care'. She then immediately saw that the boy's attitudes were invalidating this core construct. When I visited four weeks later she said very simply that there was no longer a problem. It was now just a difficulty.

Alternative constructions

It follows from my observations in the preceding section that the resolution of problems and difficulties usually calls for a change in the way that they are understood. And this includes an understanding of the child's 'sense of self' and circumstances. This is not as simple as it may seem. Alternative understandings are unlikely to be arrived at, let alone be acceptable, without exploring the referrer's existing ways of making sense and awareness of how they see themselves. Eventually ideas may need to be put forward propositionally. For example 'What would happen if?' The response to that question may then indeed open the door to further explorations. It is an added advantage that the very exercise of exploring alternative constructions may lead to a change in the existing attitudes and perceptions which the referrer has of the child. Changes in action may then also follow. But how to arrive at such constructions?

Contrasts – a door to alternative constructions
The classic procedure for eliciting constructs is to ask in relation to three elements, e.g. persons, events or situations – in what important way are any two of them alike and different from the third. This leads to a dimension of understanding or appraisal which will be adjectival rather than conceptual. When this elicitation procedure is used as a prelude, for example, to completing a grid, the process can become rather mechanical. Not infrequently it leads to the difference, or contrast, pole being given either as a simple negation of the similarity pole or as a dictionary opposite. Since the essence of PCP is the personal nature of constructs, these automatic responses seem to me to be minimally meaningful. There are, however, different ways of eliciting contrasts.

Landfield (1971), in what he calls a Pyramid Procedure, abandons the requirement of three elements. Having elicited a single description of a person he then asks the subject to describe someone who is 'not like that'. In my experience this simple 'How would you describe someone not like that' demands of the subject a conscious search for language with which to verbalise his contrast. This search, and the further elaboration which it entails, often leads to material which may be very illuminating at a 'clinical' level. In this sense it then opens doors for an individual to see his or her reality, including their 'sense of self' in different ways.

I can illustrate this with an example. A lady in a workshop on the use of drawings started to cry. Not knowing quite why this should be, instead of asking why, I asked instead 'How would you describe a person who would not cry in these circumstances?' She replied that she would think all this was a waste of time. 'So you did not see it as a waste of time?' 'Oh no!' she replied and her tears abated. By way of a comment, to ask 'Why?' has an overtone of invalidating a person's right to their own reality. To ask 'What sort of a person would not' validates that right and the response can be used for further growth and development.

The story continued: the staff meeting

A meeting of this nature is always an adventure in the sense that one never knows what will happen. It is also a challenge to one's professional core constructs – can I cope? can I make sense of things? can I intervene in some way to make a difference? My basic tool is the question, underlying which is the thought, sometimes put into words, 'What would happen if?' and, pre-eminently, the further thought, 'What would arise in response to a request for a contrast?' The account which follows shows these thoughts put into action.

There were five residential social workers present. These included the unit manager and James' key workers. An administrative officer was present as an observer. I am indebted to the unit manager for very skilfully recording what happened, not infrequently verbatim, and making this available to me. Passages in double quotes are taken verbatim from this record. Passages in single quotes are my own re-wording of some of that material in order to make clear the logic of the questions. I have also numbered them in sequence.

I was able to present my earlier report on James as a basis for a comparison with the present. Currently he was suspended because of "appalling behaviour at the weekend and a refusal to attend school". At a psychological level my observation of "not giving more than the obvious" in the previous report was matched by the present statement of "his unwillingness to share any of his real feelings, i.e. not to give anything away".

My opening invitation was to look at things within a context of "Our own normative frame of reference for judging behaviour in contrast to how we might imagine James might see things." We know how we see the world, but what about James? Specifically I ask

> 'What sort of boy would behave in ways consistent with how we imagine James sees his world?' (Question 1).

Clearly, however, there are probably many boys who sees things as James does but do not behave like him. My next question is aimed to pick up this contrast:

> 'What sort of boy sees things as James does but does not behave like him?' (Question 2).

And it would be an inference that James' behaviour may well be an implicit defence against being that sort of boy. Two descriptions were given for Q1 'deeply hurt' and 're-jected' each with a description in answer to Q2. I link the two responses into single propositions.

> 'The boy who is deeply hurt (Q1) and does not behave like James'

> "would feel weak and vulnerable to others if he appeared hurt" Q2)

> 'The rejected boy (Q.1) who did not behave like James'

> "willingly accepts substitute love and care from others in place of those who should have (parents)" (Q2)

This led to an elaboration by staff members to the effect that James does not wish to be seen as other than normal in the eyes of the world. "He hates it to be known that he lives at this special residential school", i.e. accepting substitute care.

The thoughts expressed in this sequence, adding to my existing awareness, led me intuitively to pose the question: 'Could James be suicidal?' The outcome was surprising and I quote:

> "The staff unanimously agreed that some of James' thoughts, fantasies and deeds would indicate that he is at risk of this. They had recently discussed this but with each other one-to-one, perhaps afraid to share fears openly in group until now."

A further elaboration followed almost as a formulation arising from this new awareness:

> "James needs to perceive himself as having strength, power over others and superior intelligence to maintain his self-regard – if this is threatened or lost he would have nothing left."

I do not recall just how this formulation was reached. I suspect that it came from pooling a number of thoughts from different sources. It certainly seems very apt.

My next question followed psychologically from this and hinged on seeing behaviour as a way of surviving. "What sort of a boy is likely to display behaviour like James' as a way of surviving?" (Question 3) with the follow-up question "What sort of boy would have had such experiences and not behave like James?" (Question 4). Again there were two descriptions: "has been abused (emotionally)" and "unloved". Once more I link the responses into single propositions.

'A boy who has been abused emotionally (Q3) and did not behave like James'

would be

"a victim, compliant, a doormat'"(Q4)

'A boy who has been unloved (Q3) and did not behave like James'

"might be withdrawn or seek love from others rather than hide it, try to be popular, loveable" (Q4)

If these two Q4 responses, taken in juxtaposition, were to be valid alternatives for James it would not perhaps be surprising that he should defend himself against them, e.g. the possibility of falling into a state of homosexual dependency.

At this point I again raised the issue of potential suicide and the formal action that should be taken, e.g. bringing this to the attention of those in authority. And then more surprise. I quote:

"The possible danger to others should be noted regarding the observation that James is always testing his limits (like a small child would). This has implications for his safety, does he believe he is invincible? Links with fantasy – belief in UFOs and aliens – believing the X Files to be true."

Sadly I missed making the connection that putting himself at risk, as hinted at above, may also be consistent with a less than adequate concern for staying alive. Yet perhaps their observations reflect the possibility that some of the staff were dimly aware of this.

My next question asks "What kind of boy would see this behaviour (i.e. pushing the limits) as normal?" (Q5) with the follow up "What sort of boy like that would not behave like that?" (Q6). One response only was given 'egocentric, extending his boundaries'.

'The sort of boy who would be egocentric in this sense (Q5) but not behave like James, i.e. extending his boundaries'

"would be a boy with support systems, someone comfortable and confident with their ego" (Q6).

Perhaps this description is that of normal, healthy development in a young person, manifestly not seen to be true for James.

As a way of attempting an integration of all this material in relation to staff anxieties about James, and bearing in mind the implications for their professional and personal core constructs, I put the following key question:

'James has had an enormous investment (over 10 years) in preventing people from "getting through" or "helping". What would happen if someone broke through his barriers? What are the risks?'

There was a profound silence.

In a sense this was a challenge to social workers' core constructs of themselves as 'helping', 'understanding', and 'relating' with their charges, in particular with James. I think this was tacitly recognised. Hence the silence. I put my understanding of this silence into words by commenting on how hard it was not to try to help since 'helping' in that sense was an important aspect of how they see themselves. But there might be a danger to James and others if the negativities they had recognised underlying James' presentation of himself were to be released.

In retrospect a parallel can be recognised between the situation of James on the one hand and the staff on the other. If we were to succeed in 'breaking through' to him, what would he have left? If we were to take away the traditional view of a social worker's professional 'sense of self' as 'helping and understanding' what would she or he have left?

Clearly there was a need for some alternative way of understanding people and situations in order to make good the apparent threat to their role. The communication model of how people interact as described by Watzlawick et al. (1967) seemed very appropriate. They demonstrate how interpersonal communication always calls for a recognition of three components: content (both verbal and non-verbal), an awareness of relationships (how I see you and how I see myself), and the context in which the interaction takes place. Communication automatically involves validation, invalidation or ignoring each or any of these three components. The implications of this model were beautifully captured by the unit manager who wrote in her record her understanding of what I had suggested:

> "*Should the aim not be to break through or release trapped feelings or try to change his reality, but try to communicate with him as he is. Accept what he says whilst asking questions to check his reality – raise an eyebrow – cast a seed of doubt to make him question his own perceptions.*'"

By now I was not surprised that new suggestions from me should immediately be followed by the introduction of new material from the staff. This time it was to the effect that sometimes, just sometimes, he had shown feelings. On one occasion, while telephoning his father, tears had been seen rolling down his cheeks. He was also beginning to acknowledge female members of staff by calling them by their names. An incident was recalled in which he had 'participated spontaneously in three-way discussions with staff and peers – this was surprising and is positive'. On another occasion he had recently supported a female staff member when verbally attacked by another pupil.

This particular incident was a godsend in providing an opportunity to illustrate the use of the communication model I had just described. James' action could be acknowledged by simply saying 'Thank you for helping me'. This, at one and the same time, validates him as a person and his valuing of the staff member and the appropriateness of the context within which the event had happened.

Perhaps, after all that had been shared in the discussion, these final contributions reflected an incipient reconstruction of James and his problematic behaviour.

Final observations

Quite fortuitously my eye spotted two sentences in succeeding papers of George Kelly (see Maher, 1969, pp.8, 51). They read: 'To ask a question is to invite the unexpected.' And 'Beware of the obvious.' In retrospect it can be seen that taken together they describe the essence of this paper. I asked questions and I did not know what to expect. I guarded against the obvious by seeking contrasts. The aim of this form of enquiry was to promote the possibility that some, if not all, members of the group could begin to see things differently.

I made the point much earlier that to ask for a contrast, in the form I had used in this staff discussion, is usually to require that a person makes a conscious search for an answer. It seldom arises automatically and is seldom obvious. Moreover, it is an interesting observation that the search often brings to light material long since known and long since forgotten. Or it may lead to the making of new links and connections between old and new material. The search itself may be seen as the exercise of imagination, in the same way that it requires an act of imagination on the part of the interviewer to invent questions which will promote that end. And, arising from the joint imaginations, alternative constructions of people and events may develop. There can, however, be no guarantee of success.

If my memory serves me correctly I am led to believe that this imaginative process is also the beginnings of the scientific enterprise.

References

Landfield, A.W. (1971) *Personal construct systems in psychotherapy*. Chicago: Rand McNally.

Lunt, I., Van Meeuwen, R. & Harskamp, A. (in preparation). Personal construct psychology and the practice of educational psychology: Selected papers of Tom Ravenette.

Maher, B. (1969). Clinical psychology and personality: Selected papers of George Kelly. New York: Wiley.

Watzlawick, P., Beavin, J.H. & Jackson, D.D. (1967). Pragmatics of human communication. New York: Norton.

Volumes 16, 17 and 18 (1999–2001): Shortlisted papers

Theme consultancy – exploring organisational themes to symptomatic problems of behaviour management in a primary school
by Joan Baxter, vol 17(1), 33–50.

An analysis of the organisational constraints on educational psychologists working at the whole school level: The opportunity of inclusion
by Robert Stratford, vol 17(1), 86–97.

Changing the profile of an educational psychology service
by Sonia Sharp, Norah Frederickson and Karen Laws, vol 17(1), 98–111.

Issues in the development of a homosexual identity: Practice implications for educational psychologists
by Lucy Robertson and Jeremy Monsen, vol 18(1), 13–31).

Panel Members
Convenor: Alison Gardener, specialist senior educational psychologist, Northamptonshire
Joe Dawson, acting principal educational psychologist, Leicester City
Miriam Landor, educational psychologist, West Lothian

Introduction by the panel

The paper that our panel has selected to represent this period is *Issues in the development of a gay or lesbian identity: Practice implications for educational psychologists* by Lucy Robertson and Jeremy Monsen. We found it to be informative, enlightening, and as relevant for educational psychology practice today as it was seven years ago. Indeed, we consider it essential reading for all EPs. Although there have been some changes regarding society's response to homosexuality since this paper was written, civil marriages being one of them, the reader is soon brought to realise that issues for young people have not.

This article deepens understanding of this vulnerable grouping within our education system whose needs are often overlooked. It does this by raising our awareness about key issues concerning the psychosexual development of children and adolescents. A concise, historical account is provided of how socio-cultural influences have resulted in contemporary attitudes towards homosexuality. This is followed by a synopsis of the development of sexual identity in children and young people with a number of theories outlined. The difficulties faced by young people with developing gay and lesbian identities are explained, including reference to complex constructs such as 'internalised homophobia'. We are then led to appreciate how the attitude of family, school and peers can impact on this. The article concludes by showing how our role as EPs can make a difference both for the individual and for schools by raising their awareness and practice regarding homosexuality. Practical suggestions are sensitively offered about how we might do this. Once read and digested, any potential ignorance is addressed and replaced by an increased sense of confidence to 'tune into' the issues and respond accordingly.

Although this paper pre-dates the advent of *Every Child Matters* and the Scottish equivalent *Getting it Right for Every Child*, it fits so aptly within their scope. Its underpinning rationale is the promotion of positive mental health and emotional wellbeing whilst recognising diversity, an agenda EPs are uniquely well placed to help address within schools.

To conclude, we consider the paper to be extremely well written and researched, bearing proud testimony to the application of psychology within the profession.

Alison Gardner, Jo Dawson, Miriam Landor

Address for correspondence
Alison Gardner, 16 Eliot Close, Newport Pagnell, Bucks. MK16 8QS.
E-mail agardner@northamptonshire.gov.uk

Issues in the development of a homosexual identity: Practice implications for educational psychologists

Lucy Robertson & Jeremy Monsen

Abstract

'Sexual identity' has been defined by Savin-Williams (1995b) as '… the enduring sense of oneself as a sexual being which fits a culturally created category and accounts for one's sexual fantasies, attractions and behaviours' (p.166). This paper considers some of the ways that an individual arrives at his or her own unique sexual identity. It explores some of the implications for young people of developing a gay, lesbian or bisexual sexual identity and discusses the possible role that educational psychologists (or similar practitioners) may have in challenging some of the causes of the psychological damage endured by gay, lesbian and bisexual young people.

As Savin-Williams (1995b) observed, sexual identity is in large part a function of a 'culturally created category'. Initially, then, it is important to discuss some of the historical, political and cultural factors which have given rise to current Western categories of 'homosexual', 'lesbian' and 'gay'. Anthropological evidence from contemporary hunter-gatherer tribes and findings from earlier civilisations suggest that in many societies male bisexuality was, and continues to be, regarded as natural, and frequently played a significant role in 'rites of passage' for adolescent boys (Duberman, Vicinus & Chauncey, 1989; Norton, 1997).

The privileged status of male homosexuality within classical Greek society is well documented, and celebrated in both homoerotic art and literature (Duberman et al., 1989). The position of male homosexuality seems to have been similar within other early civilisations, including Chinese, Indian and the Islamic empire. The negative perceptions of homosexual activity which have fuelled contemporary attitudes of 'deviance and immorality' appear to stem predominantly from the Judaeo-Christian religious tradition (Duberman et al., 1989; Norton, 1997).

Many arguments still cited as evidence of the 'perverse and deviant' nature of homosexuality are found in biblical passages within the Old Testament. Such passages derive from the Hebrew view which valued male sexuality within marriage above all else, so that all other forms of sexual activity were banned. It is likely that these passages have been subjected to mistranslation and hence misinterpretation over the millennium, as many passages do in fact portray homosexual love in a positive light (for example, the tender and enduring relationship between Jonathan and David, Samuel 20, verses 41-42). The Hebrews undoubtedly classed homosexual activity as 'unclean', along with all other forms of banned sexual behaviour. It was probably when the Greek bible was translated into English in the seventeenth century that homosexual behaviour began to be perceived as an abomination.

The status of homosexuality within the early Christian church is still not clear. In some sects homosexual practices were actually favoured (e.g. Manichaeism). It is possibly the existence of sects like these which led St Augustine to associate homosexuality with heresy. The attitude of the Christian church towards homosexuality can be seen to be largely based upon the letters of St Paul. It is possible that his views were fuelled by the increasing power and influence of women within the early Christian church. Hence, he writes about the subjugation of women, as well as giving guidance on proper sexual relations. Penalties for homosexual activity varied depending upon which bishop was presiding at the time – there was no overall doctrine on sexual matters until AD313. The view that homosexuality was 'immoral and deviant' persisted, eventually being codified within Ecclesiastical laws (Norton, 1997).

By the mid-fourteenth century sexual expression, even within marriage, which was not of the 'vaginal-penetration-in-the-missionary-position', was thought to be contaminated by the devil and condemned. This new level of condemnation only served to drive homosexuality underground, and the practice continued throughout Europe at all levels of society. The rise of Puritanism in the mid-seventeenth century increased the systematic, cruel and zealous persecution of homosexuals even further (e.g. burnings at the stake) (Duberman et al., 1989).

In addition to the religious view that homosexual behaviour was deviant and immoral, state legislation also promoted the persecution of those indulging in homosexual activity. Such sanctions, it would appear, were in an attempt to preserve the social, political and ideological status quo. Despite the popular view that Ancient Rome sanctioned homosexual relationships, this acceptance was within strict boundaries (i.e. men were expected to marry, have children and then to consort with younger men teaching them the ways of the male world). Although male bisexuality was celebrated, female homosexuality was not accommodated since it was regarded as an attempt by women to usurp men. Throughout the Roman Empire, sexual dominance was regarded as an opportunity to control inferiors. A law of 226BC forbade relationships with free boys (although in reality such relationships occurred) and in AD342 the death penalty was introduced for 'passive homosexuals' (i.e. those 'taking it' as opposed to those 'giving it'). Active homosexuals were not punished as their behaviour was seen as still being acceptable within the framework of the dominant heterosexual male. Passive homo-

sexuals on the other hand were seen as being inferior and inadequate men who were acting like women and therefore were an affront to manliness.

Harsh penalties for homosexual activities in medieval Europe date from about 1350, immediately after the Black Death had claimed a third of the population. 'Sodomy' (anal intercourse) was regarded as a serious threat to re-populating Europe. In Britain specific state legislation dates from 1533 when the death penalty for 'buggery' was introduced by Henry VIII. By making this a secular rather than an ecclesiastical crime Henry hoped to weaken further the power of the church in England for his own obvious purposes (Norton, 1997).

The death penalty was finally abolished in England and Wales in 1861, and replaced by penal servitude under the new Offences Against the Person Act, including the 'Labouchere amendment'. This was the only act in Europe at the time which penalised homosexual acts in private as well as in public. It was also responsible for increasing further hostility towards homosexuals, as it conveniently played into the hands of blackmailers, with many high profile scandals and trials ensuing.

The most profound was undoubtedly the trial of Oscar Wilde in 1895. This trial marked the emergence of a specific social homosexual identity, as opposed to activities, and created stereotypes in people's minds which still linger to this day. Wilde's conviction criminalised homosexuality itself, and led to an era of increased fear for all homosexuals. During the post-war years there was a witch-hunt against many prominent homosexuals within the British establishment. Some of the residue from this period still influences contemporary thinking (Berg, 1959; Dollimore, 1991).

The atrocities committed during World War II also included the systematic extermination of Europe's homosexuals by the Nazis. Within Nazi ideology homosexual behaviour was seen as a 'perversion' and a denigration of manliness. It was during this era that the pink triangle was used to identify homosexuals, much as the yellow star was used to identify Jews. Ironically, the pink triangle has now been reclaimed as an international symbol of 'Queer Pride'. It has only been in recent years that this aspect of the war has been acknowledged. Even today many governments regard the homosexuals who died in the concentration camps as nothing more that 'common criminals' and have refused any form of recognition or compensation.

Homosexual behaviour between consenting adults was finally decriminalised within England and Wales in 1967 (i.e. consenting sexual relationships with another man over the age of 21 in private with no one else present in the dwelling! This followed the Wolfenden report, Berg, 1959). Other areas of Britain followed, with the Isle of Man being the most recent to decriminalise the offence (1992), albeit under great pressure from the European Union Parliament. The most recent legislation against homosexuality is Section 28 of the 1988 Local Government Act which prevents the 'promotion of homosexuality by local authorities'. Currently there are moves in England and Wales (at the time of writing Scotland has just repealed its legislation) to overturn and replace this law. However, such plans have caused a storm of protest with many of the arguments being aired reminiscent of the decriminalisation and the various age of consent debates (i.e. it's against nature and therefore abnormal, it's sick, it encourages child sexual abuse and makes children homosexual, and so on).

State legislation against homosexuality was often prompted by concerns about maintaining the population (i.e. if we were all homos humans would die out), protecting children and young people (i.e. these queers prey on children and make them queer) and retaining the balance of power within society. Restricting any freedom is a means of subjugating rebellious beliefs and peoples. It is possibly for this reason that those who flagrantly broke laws related to sexual conduct came to be viewed as revolutionary, rebel-

lious and most of all dangerous. Homosexuality has been linked with political extremism since the French Revolution, after which it was believed in England that revolutionaries bred sodomites. More recently homosexuality has been linked with left-wing politics (i.e. the so-called 'Cambridge homosexual mafia' of Burgess and Filby and in the United States with the McCarthy trials).

In 1970 the Gay Liberation Front (GLF) arose within the United Kingdom as part of a much wider era of social militancy against the 'old order'. Being more visible and open only confirmed in many people's minds the link between homosexuality, left-wing politics and the belief that homosexuals were a threat to the 'family and society'. The GLF was inspired by the Stonewall riots in New York in 1969, after police raided the Stonewall Inn. The Stonewall was a neighbourhood bar catering for a large 'drag queen' clientele. After years of raids by the police, payoffs and hassles a group of patrons decided enough was enough and held the police at bay for three days. The Stonewall incident represented a psychological turning point in popular gay culture – a point where gays and lesbians became more visible and much more assertive (Duberman, 1994).

GLF hailed less secretive lifestyles, and insisted on members 'coming out' publicly. Any increase in understanding and compassion towards gays and lesbians in the past 30 years is a direct result of the actions of the GLF. However, the increased publicity and political activities led to a strengthening of homophobia and prejudice. The revolutionary nature of the organisation, and close associations with extreme Marxism, caused many internal divisions, and by 1972 the organisation had fragmented into many smaller groups. Significantly, women who have often been marginalised within both straight and gay culture were the first group to distance themselves from the organisation and set up their own body.

The AIDS epidemic starting in the early 1980s triggered a huge outpouring of moral panic and hysteria against the gay commu-nity ('AIDS Carrying Scum' – graffiti on wall in central London, 1991). It was the catalyst for a revival in religious extremism, many re-garding AIDS as the just 'gay plague', God's punishment for an abhorrent lifestyle. The slow response of various governments to-wards the epidemic, in addition to the hys-terical reaction of the general community, served to re-politicise gay men in particular. It brought out a sense of solidarity and a de-sire to triumph over an indifferent and prej-udiced community (e.g. 'Silence = Death' slogan from the mid to late 1980s).

The association of homosexuality with in-sanity and sickness was not new of course. Such views are inexorably linked to history and socio-cultural prejudices (King & Bartlett, 1999). Although masturbation was linked with insanity and sickness from the beginning of the eighteenth century, it was not until the end of the nineteenth century that homosexuality came to be viewed as an individual's sexual identity, rather than a pat-tern of behaviour. Ulrichs (1825–1895, cited in Duberman et al., 1989) proposed that there were three types of foetus. As well as male and female he termed the third type 'urning' – a foetus with the physical charac-teristics of one gender, but the sexual in-stincts of the other. Ulrichs argued that although the homosexual instincts were 'ab-normal' they were inborn and therefore nat-ural. He pleaded for humane treatment on these grounds.

Once homosexuality had been identified as pathological, much time and effort was spent (and still is) looking for a cause and cure for the sexual dysfunction in all fields of medicine, psychiatry and psychology. De-spite Ulrichs' pleadings for humane treat-ment, this was not to be the case. Many approaches to treatment have been devel-oped including: hypnosis, castration, electric shock treatment, lobotomy, hormone treat-ment, life sentence in mental institutions and aversion therapy (all equally unsuccess-fully) (King & Bartlett, 1999; Savin-Williams & Cohen, 1996). Homosexuality was eventu-ally removed from the *Diagnostic and Statisti-cal Manual of Mental Illness* in 1973 (Krajeski, 1996). However, it was not until 1992 that the tenth edition of the *International Classifi-cation of Diseases* finally got rid of the term as a diagnosis (World Health Organisation, 1992). The belief that homosexuality is a pathological condition in need of a cure is, however, still prevalent within the ethos of many medical (and related) fields today.

Summary

The previous section has explored some of the socio-cultural influences which have re-sulted in contemporary attitudes towards gays and lesbians and suggests three impor-tant themes. Firstly, although contemporary attitudes arise directly from historical events and prejudices, generally homophobia seems to have increased persistently throughout history, from a time when homo-sexual behaviour was not distinguished from any other form of banned sexual behaviour (including masturbation and adultery) to the present when individuals may be perse-cuted for their sexual identity, regardless of the behaviour they indulge in.

Secondly, regardless of the harsh penal-ties against homosexuality, it has always ex-isted, either overtly or covertly depending upon the social context. Despite state and ec-clesiastical legislation there has always been a huge degree of hypocrisy in relation to im-plementation of such legislation.

Thirdly, and most importantly, is the gen-eral omission and exclusion of women from the history of homosexuality with some im-portant exceptions (Duberman et al., 1989). This omission is symptomatic not of a more liberal or understanding attitude towards women, but of the inability of many genera-tions of men (and women) to perceive women as autonomous sexual beings, and the lack of power of women within society, meaning that their actions were not consid-ered a threat to the 'natural order'. There is currently no legislation against lesbianism. There are about twenty points of law still ei-ther explicitly or by omission discriminating against the gay and lesbian community. There is a real need for more home-grown research into the experiences and needs of young lesbians.

While research in the field of psychology has explored the attitudes of individuals towards gays and lesbians, sociology has shifted the focus from the individual to concerns with the social responses to gays and lesbians. Sociologists such as Plummer (1992) have emphasised the importance of viewing gay and lesbian sexuality, not so much within the context of the individual prejudices of 'homophobics', but in terms of the much more powerful concept of 'heterosexism'. Plummer (1992) defines heterosexism as:

A diverse set of social practices in an array of social arenas, in which the homo/hetero binary distinction is at work whereby heterosexuality is privileged (p.19).

The current 'culturally created category' for a gay or lesbian identity continues to be one informed by negative stereotypes and prejudices derived from historical portrayals of gays and lesbians as deviant, immoral, sick, criminal and politically extreme. These views are held by individuals, but also continue to be sanctioned by society at large through the promotion of implicit heterosexist assumptions about the roles of men and women.

The development of sexual identity

Since the 1970s research into many aspects of gay and lesbian sexuality has proliferated, yet still even the most basic of demographic information on the gay and lesbian community is unknown. A survey conducted in the USA during the 1980s suggested that three per cent to six per cent of the male population were exclusively homosexual, with between about two per cent to three per cent of women being exclusively lesbian (Money, 1988; Savin-Williams & Cohen, 1996). One of the main limitations of research to date on gays and lesbians is that it largely neglects the experiences of lesbians in favour of gay men.

An important, yet still relatively neglected area of research, relates to the developmental processes by which individuals come to identify themselves as having a gay or lesbian orientation. Most classic works on human development have focused almost exclusively upon heterosexual experiences and patterns of development. When not omitted entirely, the existence of same-sex attractions are often acknowledged within the context of pathology or immaturity (Cox, 1983).

A growing body of research suggests that adult sexual orientation (erotic attraction to people of the same, the opposite or both genders) relates in some way to childhood gender identity (that is the ability to identify their own and others' gender) and sex-typed behaviour (or gender-role) behaviour (Green, 1987; Money, 1988). Money was the first to define 'gender role'. It refers to all those behaviours, attitudes, and personality traits that a society designates as masculine or feminine, that is, 'appropriate' for or typical of the male or female social role (Savin-Williams & Cohen, 1996).

Children usually develop an awareness of their own gender between the ages of about two and three years of age and are able to identify correctly the gender of others between the ages of about three to five. At this stage, children usually identify with a gender role (develop an awareness of an 'appropriate' sex-typed behaviour), which is then typically over-learnt (McKnight, 1997; Money, 1988).

There are many different theoretical perspectives relating to the way in which children learn about their gender. Undoubtedly the process begins very early, probably soon after conception, with 'active pregnancies' being perceived as being more male-like and 'passive pregnancies' being more female-like. Certainly within the first couple of days of a baby's birth, boys and girls are treated very differently by their parents (particularly their fathers), and different meanings are attributed to their behaviour depending upon their gender, which immediately reinforces accepted stereotypes (McKnight, 1997; Money, 1988).

Different theoretical perspectives emphasise the roles of biological, cultural, cognitive and emotional processes in influencing a child's identification with a gender role and associated sex typed behaviour (McKnight, 1997). The exact contribution of each is not yet clear, but they would most likely all play a role. Children usually begin to develop an awareness of their sexual orientation during childhood and early adolescence. At this time children are becoming sexually mature, learning facts about their bodies and sex. They begin to make sense of these facts in terms of their own desires, emotions, behaviour and relationships, and at the same time eroticise and give new meaning to familiar feelings. Through this process adolescents eventually establish an individual sexual identity.

Green (1987) found that 75 to 80 per cent of boys who showed gender atypical behaviour later developed a bisexual or homosexual identity, as opposed to 0 to 4 per cent of a control group. Despite this apparent relationship between gender role identification and later sexual orientation and identity, the nature of the relationship is still not fully understood, and some researchers remain sceptical about whether any relationship exists at all (McKnight, 1997; Money, 1988).

At least three possible models have been proposed by those researchers who maintain that a relationship does exist between gender role and sexual orientation. Green (1987) states that adult sexual orientation is the end-state of a developmental process of psycho-sexual differentiation, in which gender identity develops first, then gender role and finally orientation. Others (e.g., Isay, 1989) suggest that this sequence is reversed and that a child's sexual orientation influences the expression of sex-typed behaviour. The third model does not consider the relationship developmentally, but suggests that both sexual orientation and sex-typed behaviour are influenced by the same factors, particularly biological such as prenatal sex hormones (McKnight, 1997; Zucker, 1990).

More evidence that sexual orientation has a biological basis has been provided by Meyer-Bahlburg, Ehrhardt, Rosen, Gruen, Varidiano, Vann & Neuwalder (1995) who demonstrated that levels of prenatal oestrogen may play a role in the development of human sexual orientation, through their effect on structural sex differences within the brain (i.e. the hypothalamus). Other research indicates that a variety of factors may be related to sexual orientation. Blanchard, Zucker, Bradley & Hume (1995), for example, have demonstrated that male homosexuals have a greater than average proportion of male siblings, and a later than average birth order. As yet no sound explanation for these findings has been established. Such research highlights the need for caution in interpreting such results. It is easy to fall into the 'chop-stick' hypothesis, that is the robust finding that there is a very high correlation between having blue eyes and having difficulties using chop sticks! Rather than something biological causing such differences it is highly likely that culture plays its part. Finally, some researchers question the value of attempting to find a common and universal 'cause' of homosexuality.

> *Considering the 'varieties' of homosexuality and the variety of meanings constructed out of same-gender sexual orientation, there seems to be little value in trying to find a common origin of homosexuality. (Boxer, Cohler, Herdt & Irvin, 1993, p.255)*

A more constructive way forward may be to develop new theoretical models which 'allow' for the development of a gay or lesbian orientation as being a natural part of human diversity within the psycho-sexual differentiation process. New conceptualisations of sexual orientation may need to be developed in response to increasing evidence that, for many individuals, it is not a 'fixed' state. Improved techniques for assessing sexual orientation are necessary, particularly techniques which are sensitive to the needs and experiences of adolescents. Such advances would probably allow a more rational understanding of the experiences of young gays and lesbians from a wide variety of cultures and backgrounds.

Difficulties associated with developing a gay or lesbian identity

An increasing amount of research has been carried out in the United States investigating the experiences of young people who have come to identify themselves as gay or lesbian. This research has helped to counteract earlier work which tended to approach the study of gays and lesbians in terms of psychopathology which was assumed to be a direct result of their 'abnormal sexuality'. Research has served to show that many gay, lesbian, bisexual and transgendered adolescents lead well adjusted, satisfying and happy lives (Savin-Williams, 1995a; Savin-Williams & Cohen, 1996). Some gay and lesbian youth will obviously suffer difficulties in their social-emotional development, just like any other section of the adolescent population. Generally, however, such work highlights the growing recognition that:

> Much of the psychopathology attributed to the gay adolescent is a consequence of the stereotyping and homophobic preoccupations of their peers, teachers and parents, who do not understand the manner in which these gay and lesbian adolescents differ from others. (Boxer et al., 1993, p.258)

Despite the evidence that gay and lesbian adolescents do not differ fundamentally from their heterosexual counterparts in any respect other than their sexuality, there are still challenges in belonging to a sexual minority which, as the above quotation illustrates, can in themselves be the cause of additional stress and difficulty.

Self-acknowledgement leading to self-acceptance of sexual identity

For the youth struggling with a stigmatising sexual identity, adolescence can be a time of conflict and distress. With pressures from family and peers to be heterosexual, gay male, lesbian and bisexual youths face unique hurdles in their efforts to forge a healthy sense of self. (Savin-Williams, 1995b, p.174)

'Coming out' is the term used to describe the process by which an individual incorporates a same-gender sexual identity into their sense of self and so makes a transition to a gay or lesbian lifestyle. The usual steps in this process are firstly self-acknowledgement of their sexuality, then sharing this identity with one other person, and gradually making contacts with other gays and lesbians. In time individuals learns to accept who and what they are. Many gay and lesbian adults report that they felt 'different' from an early age. This feeling of isolation or apartness grows with age, and is given new meaning during adolescence. At this stage, many young people realise that they do not have erotic interest in the opposite sex, but are likely to reject any definition of them being 'gay, lesbian, homosexual, queer, pansy, fag, faggot, poof, poofter' and so on, which peers may have labelled them. A growing awareness that their feelings of alienation may have a sexual component, however, makes it increasingly difficult to deny same-sex attractions.

A study by Boxer et al. (1989, reported in Savin-Williams, 1995b) revealed the average age of disclosure to be about 16 years, for both boys and girls, although homosexual activity was likely to have begun at an earlier age (around 13 years for boys and about 15 years for girls). Some youth reported 'relief and joy' when they reached self-awareness, and generally there was a positive association between acknowledgement (and later acceptance) of sexual identity and feelings of self-worth. This is not the case for all young people however.

Gay and lesbian adolescents are very much aware of the prevailing attitudes held within society and in their own families towards 'queers'. Gay and lesbian adolescents are aware of one of the powerful fears, that of social rejection and isolation. Such feelings act as defences against self-recognition, and delay the process of 'coming out' to oneself and others. For young people from ethnic minorities, the difficulties posed by the task of developing a positive self-image during adolescence may be magnified because of the need to develop not only a robust gay or lesbian identity, but also a healthy ethnic identity. Such young people may be the recipients of racism, in addition to 'homophobic' prejudice (Savin-Williams & Rodriguez, 1993, in Savin-Williams, 1995b).

Particular difficulties in establishing a positive self-image may result for boys and girls who develop awareness of their gay or lesbian sexuality at an early age, since they may lack the maturity, experience and language to cope with this recognition, as well as being relatively more dependent upon their families.

Attitudes of family, school and peers
For many young people, the fear of rejection by parents appears to be well founded. A British survey (Trenchard & Warren, 1984) revealed that approximately 40 per cent of parents reacted badly to their children's disclosure. The most extreme reaction was being forced to leave home (11 per cent). Another common response was to send their son or daughter to a doctor (10 per cent) or psychiatrist (15 per cent). Research suggests that, although boys find it more difficult than girls to disclose their sexuality, parents tend to have more difficulty in accepting a daughter's lesbianism.

As well as experiencing rejection from their families, and general 'heterosexism', many young gays and lesbians receive direct abuse from prejudiced and intolerant peers. There is particular pressure to conform to certain stereotypes during adolescence and, as Gonsiorek (1988) has observed, that failure to do so can result in cruel behaviour from peers (see Rivers' paper in this edition).

> *Adolescents are frequently intolerant of differentness in others and may castigate or ostracise peers, particularly if the perceived differentness is in the arena of sexuality or sex roles. (Savin-Williams, 1995b, p.116)*

Although peers are responsible for the majority of abuse (64 per cent in a study of American college students by D'Augelli in 1992) abuse is also received from teachers and other staff in schools and colleges (this accounted for 23 per cent of the abuse experienced in the above study – see Crowley, Hallam, Harré & Lunt's paper in this edition). The majority of gay and lesbian young people appear to have received abuse at some time. In D'Augelli's (1992) study up to 72 per cent of the sample had been the recipients of either verbal or physical abuse. Trenchard and Warren's 1984 survey of London adolescent homosexuals revealed similar figures, with 58 per cent of respondents reporting verbal abuse and 21 per cent reporting having been beaten up (for gay men this figure was 27 per cent).

Another study conducted within the United Kingdom by Stonewall (Mason & Palmer, 1996) reported that 48 per cent of respondents aged under 18 experienced violence, with 90 per cent having experienced name calling because of their sexuality. Of the violent attacks reported 50 per cent involved fellow students and 40 per cent actually took place within school. These figures are high, and confirm that the fear of violence, intimidation and rejection reported by many young gays and lesbians is indeed justified.

Lack of an accepted framework in which to form relationships
As well as receiving overt hostility from some peers, many gay and lesbian young people experience more subtle difficulties in the area of peer relationships. Because of the fear of rejection and hostility, many young gays and lesbians will not have disclosed their sexuality at school or amongst friends. The term 'passing' or 'in the closet' are used to describe people who have acknowledged their sexual identity themselves, but have not disclosed it publicly. Lesbian and gay adolescents who are 'in the closet' frequently terminate same-sex friendships if erotic feelings are aroused, rather than reveal their secret.

Many consequently find other-sex friendships easier because in this way they avoid physical and sexual intimacy, and if their friendships are viewed as demonstrating heterosexual 'interest', this may enhance their status with their peers.

For those adolescents who are openly gay or lesbian, the possibility of dating somebody of the same sex is often so remote that many never consider it a realistic possibility. This is not always the case, as is seen in Fricke's (1981) book about his experiences of taking his boyfriend to the school prom. However, in most cases, gay and lesbian adolescents are presented with many problems which do not confront their heterosexual peers. Initially they face the difficulty of actually locating another gay or lesbian young person in a society where such relationships are not sanctioned. If they do find a friend or partner, they are even more susceptible to harassment from various quarters, and must accept that their relationship will never be publicly recognised or celebrated.

In fact our own experience as psychologists has shown us that such relationships are often seen as 'deviant' by teachers and parents and have been sufficient in themselves for a referral to be made to an educational psychologist. The adoption of a same-sex sexual identity, then, is likely to affect all of the important interpersonal relationships in a young person's life: with their family, their friends, peers, teachers and potential partners. The next section illustrates how such experiences can have serious consequences upon the development of self-acceptance in some gay and lesbian adolescents.

Some of the negative consequences of being a gay or lesbian adolescent

Adolescence can be a time of great anxiety for most young people. For gay, lesbian and bisexual teenagers, the stresses of adolescence are significantly increased by internal turmoil over sexual identity, the reactions of family and friends, the fear of violence and abuse and the lack of opportunity to form and experiment with meaningful same-sex friendships and relationships. As we have already highlighted, it is important to remember that by no means all young gays and lesbians experience negative consequences. Yet for a significant proportion of gay, lesbian and bisexual youth, the effects of such stressors can be detrimental to mental health, and lead to a variety of damaging outcomes.

Internalised homophobia

Perhaps the most common negative consequence of being gay, lesbian or bisexual and one which results from the 'culturally created category' of 'homosexual', is internalised homophobia. This occurs when the individual incorporates negative attitudes towards gays and lesbians as part of their own self-image. Varying degrees of internalised homophobia can result, but the most extreme form involves over-generalisation of negative feelings about their sexual orientation which encompasses the entire self image. An individual may perceive that they are really 'deviant, sick, mentally ill, emotional unstable, will never be able to sustain a long-term relationship, and have difficulty with promotion and being accepted at work'. The ultimate damage being an overwhelming sense of wishing that they could have been born straight ('If I had my life over again I wished I had been straight ... it would have made work and promotion easier ... I never felt that I belonged ... I always felt an outsider at the rugby club, the pub ... male cliques ... the pressure to pass as straight the fear of rejection losing out career wise.' Excerpt from an interview with a 40-year-old gay man).

Internalised homophobia may be overt or covert. In its covert form, internalised homophobia leads to self criticism and self doubt in the face of prejudice. Discrimination is frequently tolerated, and may extend to critical and irrational views of other members of the lesbian and gay community. Overt internalised homophobia is more destructive, and probably accounts for most of the mental health problems seen within the gay and lesbian community. Overt internalised homophobia takes the form of extreme self-hatred. This can result in depression and self-destructive behaviour, such as substance abuse and suicide.

> *I lie awake tense and dream that there are others like me out there – young men like myself who I can talk with, laugh with, do things with, be myself with. What about at school? But Mum and Dad must never know, never. I know what they would do. Why can't I find other's like me to talk to, to be with, I'm lost, am I going to be alone for ever. Will I ever meet someone like me to love or will I end up like Quentin Grisp destined to a life of loneliness and rejection, a pathetic Queer. (An extract from a 1977 suicide letter of a young gay male aged 18 years who attempted to kill himself).*

The rate of completed suicides among gay and lesbian young people is unknown, as is the percentage of gay and lesbian adolescents of the total number of completed youth suicides. Although a review of research by Gibson (1989, reported in Savin-Williams & Cohen, 1996) suggests that they could account for as many as 30 per cent. This finding is supported by Remafedi, Farrow & Deisher (1993) and Trenchard and Warren (1984) who report that between 20 per cent and 30 per cent of young gay men have attempted suicide (also see Walker's paper, this issue).

Hershberger and D'Augelli (1995) found that self acceptance was the single best predictor of current and future mental health among lesbian, gay and bisexual youths, rather than level of victimisation or level of family support. However, perceived victimisation and negative family support were associated with suicides or attempted suicides in gay and lesbian adolescents. Hershberger and D'Augelli concluded:

> *A general sense of personal worth, coupled with a positive view of their sexual orientation, appears to be critical for the youths' mental health. (p.72)*

Responses to rejection and victimisation
Most adolescents can usually rely upon the support and understanding of their family and friends when they experience feelings of self doubt and anxiety. For many young gays and lesbians, this 'buffer' zone of family support is not so readily available. This leaves them more susceptible to their own negative self-talk, and also to the effects of victimisation by peers, teachers and others. The experience of rejection by family and peers can have very damaging and long lasting effects on gay and lesbian adolescents. As well as the direct consequences of victimisation by peers, Martin and Hetrick (1988, reported in Savin-Williams, 1995b) found that such experiences can lead to poor school performance, behavioural and emotional difficulties (both acting out and withdrawing), truancy, or dropping out of school altogether.

School related problems can have damaging consequences, as young gays and lesbians will be unable to fulfil their academic aspirations, which will affect later employment, social and life opportunities. One of the most extreme reactions to rejection by peers, especially when accompanied by family rejection, is running away. In some cases, gay, lesbian and bisexual adolescents may actually be compelled to leave home. In Trenchard and Warren's (1984) study 11 per cent of the sample reported that they had been thrown out of their homes. These young people, and those who run away from home, are obviously particularly vulnerable.

Martin and Hetrick (1988) found that American adolescents in this situation were at increased risk of substance abuse, prostitution and suicide. The situation within the United Kingdom is very similar, and Trenchard and Warren (1994) observe that many of these young people remain homeless as they are not seen as a priority for housing. Homeless adolescents are likely to be involved in criminal activity, but the real dangers lie in their involvement in prostitution (i.e. 'rent-boys') which in turn puts them at risk of contracting AIDS and other sexually transmitted diseases, and of sexual abuse and assault. Accurate statistics related to the number of homeless gay and lesbian adolescents involved in prostitution are not available, but it is likely to be a significant proportion of those (11 per cent) who are thrown out of their homes.

Difficulties in forming relationships
Whilst many young gays and lesbians are involved in satisfying relationships (Boxer et al., 1993; Trenchard & Warren, 1984) many lesbian, gay and bisexual adolescents encounter great difficulties which may result in damaging consequences. The separation of what these young people feel is erotic, from what is seen as socially and emotionally acceptable, can increase self doubt and cause anger and resentment, compounding negative self perceptions. Distortion of development during adolescence may occur if young people are not able to give expression to their sexuality, since sexuality provides far more than instinctual satisfaction: It is a means of dealing with and expressing feelings of love, caring and support. If adolescents are not able to explore some of the implications of their sexuality, they may develop a misperception about the nature of intimacy and relationships.

For those who have acknowledged their sexual identity, but are unable to find opportunities to date other young gays or lesbians, a common response is to seek alternative sexual encounters. Adolescent gays and lesbians (particularly males) may seek out specific public places (i.e. toilets, parks and so forth) in search of sex if they are not able to form romantic relationships. This may result in inappropriate sexual partners (i.e. abuse by older men), and an increased risk of catching AIDS and other sexually transmitted diseases.

Research by Rotheram-Borus, Reid, Rosario, Van Rossen & Gillis (1995) has found that gay and lesbian young people may follow fundamentally different developmental pathways from heterosexual youths with respect to their sexual behaviour. Whilst in heterosexual youths increased sexual behaviour is often associated with other risk taking behaviour, in gay and lesbian youth this may not be the case

(Jessor & Jessor, 1977). Their sexual behaviour is not linked to other 'problem' behaviours in the same way, and therefore appears to be more a result of circumstances. As well as the risks directly associated with casual sexual encounters, there are also less direct consequences. Young gays and lesbians may lack the opportunity to explore and develop affection and intimacy, and this can have serious consequences for relationships in adulthood.

Summary
In summary, gay and lesbian adolescents are more likely to experience different types of stressors and difficulties than their heterosexual counterparts. This is mainly due to the stigma attached to developing a gay or lesbian identity. Such pressures make the task of developing a positive self-image more challenging for most gay and lesbian young people. This fact, in addition to the extra stress caused by family attitudes, victimisation and ostracism by peers, puts gay, lesbian and bisexual adolescents at significantly greater risk of depression and suicide, as well as forcing them into situations where they are particularly vulnerable to many other risk factors. For these reasons, the well-being of gay and lesbian young people should be an important consideration for all those who work with them, including educational psychologists.

Issues in assessment and intervention
It is difficult to assess someone's sexuality other than through candid self-report. Individual sexual identities appear to exist along a continuum from exclusively same-sex to exclusively opposite-sex attraction, and do not necessarily remain in the same part on the continuum throughout a person's lifetime. Another important factor to consider is that, as Remafedi et al. (1992) found, homosexual sex is not the exclusive domain of people who self identify as bisexual, lesbian or gay, and there are also people who adopt a same sex orientation without same sex activity. Another difficulty in assessing sexuality is that many people do not publicly declare their

sexual identity for obvious reasons (i.e. rejection, abuse and so on).

The extent to which it is necessary or ethical to 'assess' sexual identity, especially that of adolescents, is highly questionable. In the past, assessment of sexuality has often resulted in sexual orientation becoming the focus of consultation, rather than the presenting problem such as feelings of rejection or depression. This has led to interventions designed to modify sexuality. Attempts have been made to justify clinical intervention around sexual orientation in order to eliminate peer ostracism, to treat underlying psychopathology, and to prevent homosexuality and transsexualism in adulthood (Savin-Williams & Cohen, 1996).

In the authors' experience it has been very rare for issues of sexuality to be used by teachers or psychologists as possible hypothesis to help explain emotional or behavioural difficulties. In most cases 'safer' within–person or family based hypotheses have been offered (i.e. learning or emotional difficulties, poor parenting and so on).

The two most common forms of 'treatment' are behaviour therapy and psychotherapy. There is little evidence, however, for the effectiveness of either treatment approach. Green (1987) found that the proportion of 'feminine' boys in his study who went on to develop gay sexual identities did not differ as a function of involvement in therapy. However, the boys who had been involved in therapy had higher self concept scores as adults, and looked back favourably on the treatment experience. This suggests that, whilst treatment appears powerless in interrupting or changing the development of sexual identity, it can be successful in increasing the development of self acceptance (King & Bartlett, 1999).

Although there are many ethical reasons not to assess sexuality, the fact remains that many young people are referred to psychologists and psychiatrists by their parents and schools, due to concerns about their gender identity or sexual orientation. There are many more young people who are referred

due to emotional or behavioural problems which could be related to their developing sexual identity. For these adolescents it is important that practitioners are aware of the possible contributions of internalised homophobia and other negative responses (i.e. school environment and ethos, peer group, family attitude) to sustaining the presenting difficulties which the young person brings.

Many more young people, however, may suffer the negative consequences of society's responses to gay and lesbian identities without ever consulting a doctor, psychiatrist, psychologist or counsellor. For these young people, assessment of their sexual orientation is not an issue. Intervention needs to take the form of raising understanding and awareness about sexuality within the educational and psychological communities in order to challenge the many untested and irrational assumptions being made about gays and lesbians.

It is, in the final analysis, homophobia and heterosexism which contribute much to the unnecessary suffering that gay and lesbian young people experience. It is argued that interventions by educational psychologists need to be related to reducing the negative experiences of young gays and lesbians and need to take place at a number of different levels within the educational establishment (i.e. individual, group and systemic levels).

The response of educational psychology services
Educational psychology services and all the individuals within them need to ensure that they are fully aware of the issues related to psycho-sexual development in childhood and adolescents and that they have developed appropriate policies and codes of practice. But above all educational psychologists need to demonstrate competence in working with sexuality issues in children and young people. As yet, the Association of Educational Psychologists and The British Psychological Society have not issued any guidelines or discussion papers (though, see Comely, 1993). The practice of heterosexism is not confined to any

specific portion of society. All social institutions can and frequently do communicate bias, mostly in subtle ways. It is important that psychologists and educational psychology services recognise that they too are liable to this form of prejudice, and need to take steps to reduce the risk of discrimination much as they now do around issues of racism, gender and disability.

Further local research

Far too little is still known about the experiences of gay and lesbian young people within the United Kingdom. More locally based primary research is needed, particularly to widen our knowledge of issues including a more representative sample of the population, especially women, ethnic minorities and those living in more rural locations within the United Kingdom. Such research will help to inform the development of responses and services for young gays and lesbians. Research by educational psychologists could be particularly useful in serving to link interventions from health and social services departments with those from educational institutions. This would enable a far more comprehensive response to the needs of gay and lesbian adolescents.

Working with individual young people, their families and teachers

There is little or no information available regarding the incidence of requests for consultation or referrals to educational psychology services for gay and lesbian adolescents, and little in the way of specific recommendations for suitable interventions (although a paper by Monsen is currently in preparation). It is unlikely (although not unknown) that a pupil will be referred to the educational psychology service due to concerns regarding their sexual identity. Educational psychologists are perhaps more likely to encounter gay and lesbian adolescents who have been referred due to concerns regarding their behaviour, emotional well-being or schoolwork.

When adolescents are referred due to concerns about self acceptance, behaviour

or a sudden decline in school work, it is essential that educational psychologists are open to the possibility that sexual identity may be a relevant aspect of the presenting difficulties, even if this is not explicitly mentioned (Monsen, Graham, Frederickson & Cameron, 1998). Some adolescents may not yet have fully acknowledged their sexuality and would therefore be unlikely to disclose it to anybody else. In this case an educational psychologist would not know the extent to which it is associated with the difficulties the young person is experiencing. Other adolescents may disclose their sexual identity to an educational psychologist, in which case the psychologist must be sensitive to issues of confidentiality, especially as in some cases the pupil will not yet have 'come out' to their family, school staff or peers.

Some young people may be open about their sexuality and the role that their sexual identity plays in the range of difficulties they are currently experiencing. In any of these cases, being gay or lesbian cannot itself be seen as a problem dimension any more than ethnicity, gender or any other personal attribute which can lead to discrimination and prejudice. Whilst not regarding sexual identity as a problem aspect in itself, it is important that educational psychologists are aware of the unique pressures and problems which are associated with developing a gay or lesbian sexual identity.

The problem most likely to be responsible for emotional or behavioural difficulties in gay and lesbian adolescents would be internalised homophobia. This is likely to manifest itself through poor self-image and low self-acceptance. In terms of interventions at an individual level, evidence suggests that working with gay and lesbian adolescents to increase their feelings of self-worth is more likely to reduce self-destructive attitudes and behaviour. Educational psychologists are unlikely to have the time to work closely with one pupil over an extended period, so it is vital that they work carefully through those adults who have daily contact with the adolescent to develop supportive groups (i.e. after school homework support groups are a good example – see Crowley, Hallam, Harré & Lunt's paper in this edition). Educational psychologists can assist individuals by providing access to information and services designed for young gays and lesbians such as youth groups and helplines.

For educational psychologists, the most effective way of increasing the self-acceptance of individual pupils is to consider the whole ethos of a school, and so assist the young person to become more accepted by their teachers and peers. The next section discusses whole school interventions.

Working with educational institutions
Much of the prejudice, discrimination and victimisation which leads to many of the difficulties associated with developing a same-sex sexual identity are encountered at school. Many schools do very little to counter such experiences either directly through mentoring, counselling and equal opportunities policies, or indirectly through the curriculum and general ethos of the school (Douglas, Warwick, Kemp & Whitty, 1997). In fact the authors' experience has been that most schools either ignore such issues or react in predictably negative ways.

Many schools use Section 28 of the 1988 Local Government Act as justification for their failure to address issues of homosexuality within their schools. This section of the Act demands that a local authority must not 'promote homosexuality' or 'promote the teaching in any maintained school of the acceptability of homosexuality as a pretend family relationship'. However, the Department of Education and Science circular 12/88 points out that 'Section 28 does not affect the activities of school governors nor of teachers. It will not prevent the objective discussion of homosexuality in the classroom, nor the counselling of students concerning their sexuality'.

This information was reiterated in the DES circular (5/94). Manchester City Council's guide to Section 28 for workers in the Education Service also points out that no court

has yet defined exactly what 'promoting homosexuality' entails, but that legal advisers suggest it would involve 'encouraging people who are not homosexual to become lesbian or gay' (p.3). Promoting equal treatment, and understanding of the needs of this minority group cannot therefore be regarded as 'promoting homosexuality'. More recently the DfEE (1999) clearly states:

> *The emotional distress caused by bullying in whatever form – be it racial, or as a result of a child's appearance, behaviour or special educational needs, or related to sexual orientation – can prejudice school achievement, lead to lateness or truancy and in extreme cases end in suicide …*
> *Head teachers have a legal duty to take measure to prevent all forms of bullying among pupils. All teaching and non-teaching staff, including lunchtime supervisors, should be alert to signs of bullying and act promptly and firmly.*
> *(DfEE, 1999, p.24-25)*

It is important then that schools are aware that their activities are not as restricted as they might have believed, and educational psychologists should work with schools to ensure that the needs of gay and lesbian students are fully met. Of the students who participated in Trenchard and Warren's (1984) study, 60 per cent said that homosexuality had never been mentioned in any lessons at school, and only five per cent said that their school library had stocked any useful books on the subject.

Educational psychologists can work to improve provision for gay and lesbian pupils through providing advice, consultation, individual, group and family-based work and training related to:
- raising awareness among school staff, governors and parents of the needs and difficulties of sexual minority students;
- developing comprehensive equal opportunities and pastoral care policies which challenge homophobia and intolerance;
- addressing pupils' needs through sex

education lessons and the general curriculum;

- supporting pupils through the availability of relevant literature; and
- encouraging the school to work with available support groups.

In this way educational psychologists can work with school staff to ensure that not only the needs of gay and lesbian pupils are catered for, but also that other pupils are less likely to develop prejudiced and intolerant attitudes and beliefs.

Conclusion

The very real concerns of gay and lesbian children and adolescents have only recently been publicly aired and discussed. Research from the United States has provided much information about the experiences of American gay and lesbian adolescents, but much of this now needs to be replicated and extended within the United Kingdom and Europe and related to the development of rational policies and services.

Educational psychologists have much to contribute to the growing understanding of adolescent sexuality. Through action research educational psychologists can find out more about the experiences and needs of Britain's gay and lesbian young people.

Educational psychology services are in a unique position of being able to bridge the gap between the services provided by public health and social services agencies and educational institutions, thus ensuring that these combine to meet the needs of gay, lesbian and bisexual youth.

By working closely with agencies specifically devoted to meeting the needs of young gays and lesbians, educational psychologists can provide individuals with opportunities to gain further advice, information and support. Within schools, educational psychologists can raise awareness of important issues, challenge attitudes and practices and discuss how schools may best respond to these at individual, group and systems levels. It is possibly through this later approach that educational psychologists can do most to increase the positive experiences of developing a lesbian, gay or bisexual identity.

Address for correspondence

Dr Jeremy Monsen, Educational Psychology Group, Psychology Department, University College London, Gower Street, London WC1E 6BT.
E-mail: j.monsen@ucl.ac.uk.

References

Berg, C. (1959). *Fear, punishment, anxiety, and the Wolfenden report*. London: George Allen & Unwin.

Blanchard, R., Zucker, K., Bradley, S., & Hume C. (1995). Birth order and sibling sex ratio in homosexual male adolescents and probably pre-homosexual feminine boys. *Developmental Psychology, 31*(1), 22–42.

Boxer, A.M., Cohler, B.J., Herdt, G. & Irvin, F. (1993). Gay and lesbian youth. In P.H. Tolan & B.J. Cohler (Eds.) *Handbook of clinical research and practice with adolescents*. New York: Wiley.

Comely, L. (1993). Lesbian and gay teenagers at school: How can educational psychologists help? *Educational and Child Psychology, 10*(3), 22–24.

Cox, K. (1983). Sex, adolescents and schools. In G. Lindsay (Ed.) *Problems of adolescents in secondary schools* (pp.126–160). London & Canberra: Croom Helm.

Department for Education and Employment (1999). *Social exclusion: Pupil support* (circular 10/99). London: DfEE.

D'Augelli, A. (1996). Enhancing the development of lesbian, gay, and bisexual youths. In E.D. Rothblum & L.A. Bond (Ed.) *Preventing heterosexism and homophobia*. California, Thousand Oaks: Sage.

D'Augelli, A. (1992). Lesbian and gay male undergraduate experiences of harassment and fear on campus. *Journal of Interpersonal Violence, 7*, 383–395.

Douglas, N., Warwick, I., Kemp, S. & Whitty, G. (1997). *Playing it safe: Responses of secondary school teachers to lesbian, gay and bisexual pupils, bullying, HIV and AIDS education and section 28*. Health and Education Research Unit, Institute of Education, University of London.

Dollimore, J. (1991). *Sexual dissidence: Augustine to Wilde, Freud to Foucault.* Oxford: Clarendon Press.

Duberman, M. (1994). *Stonewall.* New York: Plume.

Duberman, M., Vicinus, M. & Chauncey, G. (Ed.) (1989). *Hidden from history: Reclaiming the gay and lesbian past.* New York; Meridian.

Fricke, A. (1981). *Reflections of a rock lobster: A story about growing up gay.* Boston: AlyCat Books

Gonsiorek, J.C. (1988). Mental health issues of gay and lesbian adolescents. *Journal of Adolescent Health Care, 9,* 114–122.

Green, R. (1987). *The sissy boy syndrome and the development of homosexuality.* London: Yale University Press.

Hershberger, S.K. & D'Augellia, A.R. (1995). The impact of victimisation on the mental health and suicidality of lesbian, gay and bisexual youths. *Developmental Psychology, 31*(1), 65–74.

Isay, R.A. (1989). *Being homosexual: Gay men and their development.* New York: Farrar Straus Giroux.

Jessor, R. & Jessor, S.L. (1977). *Problem behaviour and psychosocial development: A longitudinal study of youth.* New York & London: Academic Press.

King, M. & Bartlett, A. (1999). British psychiatry and homosexuality. *British Journal of Psychiatry, 175,* 106–113.

Krajeski, J. (1996). Homosexuality and the mental health professions. A contempoarary history. In R.P. Cabaj & T.S. Stein (Eds.) *Textbook of homosexuality and mental health* (pp.17–31). Washington, DC: American Psychiatric Press.

Manchester City Council (1992). *Section 28 of the Local Government Act: A guide for workers in the education service.* Manchester City Council.

Martin, A. & Hetrick, E. S. (1988). The stigmatization of the gay and lesbian adolescent. *Journal of Homosexuality, 15,* 163–184.

Mason, A. & Palmer, A. (1996). *Queer bashing: A national survey of hate crimes against lesbians and gay men.* London: Stonewall.

McKnight, J. (1997). Straight science: Homosexuality, evolution and adaptation. London & New York: Routledge.

Meyer-Bahlburg, H., Ehrhardt, A., Rosen, L., Gruen. R., Veridiano, N., Vann, F. & Neuwalder, F. (1995). Prenatal estrogens and the development of homosexual orientation. *Developmental Psychology, 31*(1), 12–21.

Money, J. (1988). *Gay, straight, and in-between: The sexology of erotic orientation.* Oxford: Oxford University Press.

Monsen, J. J., Graham, B., Frederickson, N. & Cameron, S. (1998). Problem analysis and professional training in educational psychology: An accountable model of practice. *Educational Psychology in Practice, 13*(4), 234–249.

Norton, R. (1997). *The myth of the modern homosexual: Queer history and the search for cultural unity.* London & Washington: Cassell.

Plummer, J. (Ed.) (1992). *Modern homosexualities: Fragments of lesbian and gay experience.* London and New York: Routledge.

Remafedi, G., Farrow, J. & Deisher, R. (1993). Risk factors for attempted suicide in gay and bisexual youth. In L.D. Garnets & D. Kimmel (Eds.) *Psychological perspectives on lesbian and gay male experiences.* New York: Columbia University Press.

Rotheram-Borus, M.J., Reid, H., Rosario, M., Van Rossem, R. & Gillis, R. (1995). Prevalence, course and predictors of multiple problem behaviours among gay and bisexual male adolescents. *Developmental Psychology, 31*(1), 75–85.

Savin-Williams, R.C. & Cohen, K.M. (1996). *The lives of lesbians, gays, and bisexuals: Children to adults.* Fort Worth: Harcourt Brace.

Savin-Williams, R.C. (1995a). An exploratory study of pubertal maturation timing and self esteem among gay and bisexual male youths. *Developmental Psychology, 31*(1), 56–64.

Savin-Williams, R.C. (1995b). Lesbian, gay male and bisexual adolescents. In A.D'Augelli & C. Patterson (Eds.) *Lesbian, gay and bisexual identities over the lifespan.* New York: OUP.

Savin-Williams, R.C. (1990). *Gay and lesbian youth: Expressions of identity.* Washington DC: Hemisphere.

Trenchard, L. & Warren, H. (1984). *Something to tell you.* London: London Gay Teenage Group.

World Health Organisation (1992). *The ICD-10 classification of mental and behavioural disorders.* Geneva: WHO.

Zucker, K. J. (1990). Gender identity disorders in children: Clinical descriptions and natural history. In R. Blanchard & B.W. Steiner (Eds.) *Clinical management of gender identity disorders in children and adults* (pp.1–23). Washington, DC: American Psychiatric Press.

Volumes 19, 20 and 21 (2002–04): Shortlisted papers

Growing up in poverty as a developmental risk: Challenges for early intervention
by Hans Weiss, vol 21(1), 8–19.

Educational psychology and difficult behaviour in schools: Conceptual and methodological challenges for an evidence-based profession
by Andy Miller and Zazie Todd, vol 19(3), 82–95.

Consulting with children and young people: Young people's views of a psychological service
by Richard Woolfson and Michael Harker, vol 19(4), 35–46.

Ethics, professionalisation and the future landscape of educational psychology
by Alec Webster and Ingrid Lunt, vol 19(1), 97–107.

Panel Members
Convenor: Peter Wiggs, principal educational psychologist, South Gloucestershire
Sue Fairhurst, senior educational psychologist (early years), South Gloucestershire
Sheila Leech, educational psychologist, South Gloucestershire
Deborah Middleton, educational psychologist, South Gloucestershire

Introduction by the panel

We were unanimous in choosing the article by Richard Woolfson and Michael Harker, as best meeting the criteria laid down for the exercise.

The article describes a small scale study, using a focus group method, to elicit the views of eight young people aged 12–15 years, about the service they had received from the Renfrewshire Psychological Service. The study was completed as part of the best value review of the service and in line with 'current views on consulting with children'.

The panel chose this article for a number of reasons. First of all it seemed immediately relevant now, six years on from when it was first published. Now we engage in participation with children and young people but still grapple with how best to involve them and for what purpose. The article is very well written. It is concise and accessible, reflecting good EP research practice in the field. It draws on research in support of the chosen method but without introducing unnecessary complexity.

The article exemplifies an open service culture, which has grappled with that perennial question challenging EP practice, 'who is the client?' This was a challenge in 2002 and continues to be a challenge today. The findings that some children and young people didn't know why they'd been referred struck a chord with our panel. The recommendation that EP reports should be shared with the young person first before circulation to others and that they should receive a personal copy, was an unexpected outcome.

Participants' comments were analysed and categorised according to issues surrounding: the initial contact, interaction with the psychologist, written reports, outcomes and other ways of accessing the psychological service. Copious quotes were used to illustrate the key findings from the focus group discussions. Again the panel were impressed by the clarity of this section, with the analysis of the focus group discussions providing a clear framework to illuminate the emerging picture, using participants' views to good effect.

The panel began to reflect on the effect the paper had had on them and on what we might do differently as a result. We asked the question: why is it difficult for us to engage in participation with children and young people? Responses such as other people's perceptions of our role, lack of time and pressure of work seem rather feeble as I sit and write them here. We agreed the need to work to encourage our service to be more reflective and to have the courage to accept feedback – good and bad from young people – which would result from engaging in a similar exercise.

This excellent paper will serve us well as a model for consulting with children and young people about their views of our service.

Peter Wiggs, Sue Fairhurst, Sheila Leech, Deborah Middleton

Address for correspondence
Peter Wiggs, Principal Educational Psychologist, Department for Children and Young People, Bowling Hill, Chipping Sodbury, South Gloucestershire BS37 6JX.
E-mail: Peter.Wiggs@southglos.gov.uk

Consulting with children and young people: Young people's views of a psychological service

Richard Woolfson & Michael Harker

Abstract

In line with current views on consulting with children and as part of the best value review of the Renfrewshire Psychological Service, eight young people (aged 12–15 years) consented to take part in a focus group in order to explore their views of the service. Each of the participants had recent contact with an educational psychologist. The focus group discussion centred around established performance indicators used to assess the quality of service provided to children and young people by a psychological service. The results of the focus group deliberations demonstrated that Renfrewshire Psychological Service complies with all established performance indicators, with the exception of providing satisfactory written explanatory leaflets for young people. In addition, the young people taking part in the focus group suggested possible new directions for the psychological service, including a walk-in self-referring facility located in secondary schools, and access to written reports. The value of this methodology as a means for consulting with children is discussed.

Legislation

Current legislation highlights the legal requirement for professionals to consult with children about matters which have an impact on them. The United Nations Convention on the Rights of the Child, which was adopted by the United Nations in 1989 and ratified by the UK government in 1991, states that:

> *parties shall assure to the child who is capable of forming his or her own views the right to express those views freely in all matters affecting the child, the views of the child being given due weight in accordance with the age and maturity of the child.*

In Scotland, this principle is given further weighting by the Children (Scotland) Act 1995 which also takes into account the obligations under the European Convention on Human Rights. This Act specifies that all children who can form their views on matters affecting them have the right to express those views if they wish; it also specifies that children should always be consulted when major decisions are to be made about their future, whether by parents, the local authority or by the courts.

The Children (Scotland) Act 1995 additionally introduces a framework for assessment, services and support to children with disabilities and their families, and indicates that children should be 'actively involved in assessments, decision-making meetings, case reviews and conferences' and they 'should be given help to express their views and wishes and to prepare written reports and statements for meetings where necessary'. Consulting with children, therefore, is not simply the preferred model but is instead a requirement placed upon professionals working with children and young people.

Since the Act places responsibilities on local authorities to take into account the views of children who are either currently using or receiving services or who have previously received services when drawing up the children's service plans (the overall local authority plan for all services relating to children and their families), any evaluation of a local authority psychological service should seek the views of children who use the service.

Best value review

Best value is a commitment in the Scottish Executive's Programme for Government. It seeks to improve local government perform-ance in the delivery of services to local com-munities. Best value aims to ensure that the cost and quality of these services are of a level acceptable to local people by, *inter alia,* specifically increasing the role of local peo-ple in deciding the priorities for local gov-ernment services. The significance of best value in Scotland was underlined in 2000 by Wendy Alexander (then Minister for Com-munities), who confirmed that 'Best value has a crucial role in the modernisation agenda. It involves new ways of thinking and working.'

The Renfrewshire Psychological Service was selected by Renfrewshire Council to un-dergo a best value review during academic session 2001–2002. As part of this process, a focus group was established to consult with young people who had had recent contact with the psychological service.

Focus group methodology

Robson (2000) defines a focus group as:

a type of semi-structured interview carried out in a group setting. It has been much used in market research, including recently that carried out by political parties in developing policies. It is a widely used method in needs analysis but can be useful for several evaluative purposes … The main benefit of group interviews is the possibility of additional insights being gained through the interaction of ideas and suggestions from group members (p. 93).

Stewart and Shamdasani (1998) advise that an appropriate use of focus groups is to as-certain the views of products, programmes, services and other institutions – this, there-fore, makes it a suitable tool for use in a best value review. Focus groups are similar to in-dividual semi-structured interviews in that they follow a predetermined set of questions, but they provide 'value added' because, un-like individual interviews, additional ideas, suggestions and observations can arise from the dynamic interaction that occurs in a group discussion; that group dynamic can manifest itself in a direct discussion among participants or simply in one participant hearing what another has to say on a particu-lar topic and then having sufficient confi-dence to make an individual contribution.

Focus groups have been used to investi-gate the views of children and young people across a broad range of issues. For example, Charlesworth and Rodwell (1997) used this technique with children to evaluate a sexual abuse prevention programme; James (1996) to understand their views on school nutri-tion programmes; Mee (2001) to examine children's perspectives on motivation during learning; Nelson-Gardell (2001) to learn how sexually abused children perceive support services; Horner (2000) to clarify children's understanding of health and ill-ness; and Jirojanakul and Skevington (2000) to develop a 'quality of life' children's rating scale.

Focus groups with children have also been employed extensively by Children in Scotland, a national agency for voluntary, statutory and professional organisations and individuals working with children and their families in Scotland, when ascertaining the views of children and young people. For in-stance, Children in Scotland (2001) ex-plored children's views, experiences and characterisations of science both in and out of school, and the organisation is currently researching into the importance of arts and cultural awareness in the life of all children, using focus group methodology (see www.childreninscotland.org.uk). Advice on ethical issues concerning focus groups for children and young people is provided by Morgan and Scannell (1998) and Vaughn et al. (1996).

Invitation to participate

As part of the best value review of Renfrew-shire Psychological Service, potential partici-pants for the young person's focus group

were selected using the criteria that they:
- were 12–15 years old;
- were attending a secondary school in Renfrewshire; and
- had had contact with a psychologist within the previous three months;
- had been assessed by the case psychologist as having the personal and social skills needed to cope with the interactions of a focus group.

Potential participants and their parents were given full information about the nature and purpose of the focus group, and were then invited to take part. Verbal and written consent was obtained from every participant and their parents.

Focus group membership

The focus group consisted of eight young people (five boys and three girls) who met the selection criteria. This resulted in a mixture of original referral difficulties. To help maintain confidentiality and privacy, all participants attended different schools. The young people were advised clearly that during the discussions disclosure of the reason for their having contact with the psychological service would not be permitted.

The focus group was held in the Psychological Service Centre, Paisley, one morning in February 2002. Each participant was collected by individual private taxi from school and brought to the centre. When the focus group had finished, each participant received a £10 gift voucher and was then returned by individual private taxi to school.

In the room in which the focus group took place, the young people and the two moderators (depute principal psychologists) sat round a large rectangular table. Participants and moderators wore name-tags and were introduced to each other at the start of the meeting.

Proceedings were recorded by two small ATR97 desktop microphones which led into a stereo tape-recorder. In addition, the discussions were recorded manually by a note-taker who did not sit at the table and who did not take part at all in the discussions. Before

the focus group began, the young people were made fully aware once again of the recording and note-taking arrangements. Light refreshments and snacks were available. The focus group ran for approximately 30 minutes, then stopped for a short break, and then resumed for approximately a further 30 minutes.

The role of each moderator in the focus group, as generally described by Vaughn et al. (1996), included the responsibility to:
- offer concrete and unambiguous questions with illustrative examples;
- create an atmosphere in which it is acceptable to talk about negative and positive aspects;
- check regularly that the young people understood the questions being discussed;
- make the participants feel comfortable;
- ensure the participants could make comments without being judged;
- emphasise that there were no wrong answers;
- encourage participants to say what was true for them, not just to agree with others; and
- encourage participants to respond to each other's comments, not only to the moderator.

Performance indicators (PIs) for the psychological service

PIs for assessing the quality of service to children and young people by the psychological service have been identified by Mackay (1999) and Renfrewshire Psychological Service (1999). Table 1 lists PIs for this aspect of service delivery.

Since these PIs provide a benchmark against which a psychological service is assessed, they were taken as the basis for question 'prompts' which the moderators used to stimulate discussion in the focus group. However, they were used to steer the focus group discussion, rather than constrict or limit it. Without exception, participants were allowed to introduce new appropriate material into the discussion and to take the conversation in any relevant direction of their choosing. The moderators endeavoured to encourage dynamic contributions and innovative observations from the participants.

Results: Part 1 – an overview

The following is a summary of the comments made by the young people, as they discussed the referral process from the initial referral stage until the end of the assessment or intervention.

These comments arose in discussion either between a moderator and an individual child, or among a moderator and at least two young people, or among at least two young people themselves without a contribution from a moderator. Therefore, although the comments are presented individually for the sake of clarity, in many instances they are selected 'snapshots' of a broad-based discussion.

The group discourse was analysed and categorised according to the themes below. While some of these were predetermined by the PIs (for instance, 'psychologist's manner', 'treated seriously'), other new themes emerged spontaneously from the group discussion (for instance, 'pre-meeting anxiety', 'access to written reports', 'control'). Each of these themes – whether predetermined or innovative – was given equal status in the data analysis.

Issues surrounding the initial contact
- Notice of referral: the young people had clear recall of their first contact with the psychologist. Most had been told in advance by their parents, while one was told by the guidance teacher only moments before the first meeting.
  'My dad got a letter through the post and he told me I would be seeing them.'
  'It was a bit of a shock.'

- Prior understanding: none of the young people were given written information about the psychological service before meeting their psychologist for the first time, though several indicated this would

have been helpful because they had lots of concerns.
  'My mum gave me the letter but there were no leaflets.'
  'I wanted to know what kind of things they do and stuff like that.'

- Permission: in some instances the young people were informed before seeing the psychologist that they had a choice whether or not to continue with the process, but this did not happen in every case.
  'I was told to go [to the psychologist].'
  'I got asked if I wanted to see them.'
  'My dad said that I was going to a psychologist and that was it.'

- Psychologist's manner: in every instance, the psychologist was perceived as polite, punctual and responsive. None of the participants referred to embarrassment or social difficulties in connection with seeing a psychologist. All the young people felt that the psychologist explained the purpose of the contact at the start of the interview and most confirmed they were again asked for their approval to continue.
  'She said she had come to see me because I wasn't doing well in class.'
  'He told me who he was and why he was here.'

- Initial reaction to psychologist: the young person's reaction to meeting with the psychologist was reported as favourable.
  'I told my pal I've been to see him [the psychologist] and he's all right.'

- Privacy: all the participants were satisfied with the privacy surrounding the contact with their psychologist, and they all preferred contact to be in school rather than at home or in the psychological service's building itself.
  'I had a lot of privacy.'
  'I would prefer to be seen in school.'
  'I have a wee brother so it [home interview] wouldn't really be private.'

- Statement of confidentiality: the psychologist mentioned confidentiality at the start of the interview. Most young people could recall being told clearly who would become aware of the outcome of their involvement with the psychologist and were satisfied that this was adhered to.

  'It [confidentiality] is important because it was personal.'

  'I was told they [the psychologist] would tell my mum and my dad.'

  'I was nervous about teachers finding out but he told me they wouldn't.'

Issues surrounding the interaction with the psychologist

- Pre-meeting anxiety: most young people admitted apprehension about seeing the psychologist the first time. In every instance, however, this anxiety eased on actually meeting the psychologist and beginning the initial interview.

  'I was nervous the first time but then I was okay.'

  'At first I was nervous then after a while I was all right.'

- Relating to the psychologist: participants all commented favourably on the psychologist's manner and felt a positive relationship was quickly established.

  'I got a chance to talk.'

  'She talked to me like she was a normal person.'

  'It was just like two people talking.'

- Opportunity for self-expression: for the young people, the chance to state their own views to the psychologist was highly valued.

  'I could say about anything I wanted.'

  'You could get to say what you wanted.'

  'The psychologist talked to you like you were a bit older.'

- Treated seriously: all participants confirmed that they felt valued by the psychologist and that they also felt the psychologist listened to them. Some young people were pleased when the psychologist took case notes during the interview (as opposed to waiting until the end of the interview) because this was confirmation of the importance of the young person's views.

  'She wrote it down and made me feel I was understood.'

  'You know they are taking into account what you are saying.'

- Feedback and advice: each of the young people in the focus group were pleased to be given specific advice by the psychologist at the end of their sessions together, or during their sessions. Feedback and advice is highly valued and is seen as an important part of the interaction.

  'She told me what she thought and gave me some advice on it.'

  'I got told how to go about things.'

  'They [the psychologist] told me some good advice.'

Issues surrounding written reports

- Consultation in written reports: the participants placed considerable importance on written reports and some expressed the desire to be consulted about the content of the report before it was sent out – where this had happened, the young person commented favourably.

  'She let me see and told me what was going to happen.'

  'He asked me if I would like him to change any of it or to put anything in.'

- Access to written reports: all participants stated firmly that they felt strongly they should have sight of all written reports about them. Where this did not happen, they were satisfied if their parents explained the contents of the report to them. However, the clear preference was to have a personal copy of the actual report for themselves.

'You get to see what they [the psychologist] has written about you.'

'The psychologist talked me through it [the report].'

● Style of report: there was concern that psychological reports were not always written in an accessible style for young people; this led to a request for a modification in style of report writing.

'They use all big words.'

'Smaller words are more understandable.'

● Age for accessing written reports: while there was an acknowledgement that children vary in their levels of understanding depending on their age, there was a general consensus that children and young people should have access to written reports about themselves from around the age of 8–10 years.

'About ten when you are able to understand.'

'Start about eight because younger you don't really understand anything.'

Issues surrounding outcomes

● Impact: the participants agreed that contact with the psychologist had a positive impact on their lives. No negative effects were noted. In some instances, the young person did not notice the effect until several weeks after contact with the psychologist had ceased.

'It helped me quite a lot.'

'It was good for me.'

'Just talking to somebody made me feel better.'

● Control: the young people in the focus group particularly valued psychological interventions and advice that enabled them to take control of their own lives, rather than being dependent on the responses of others.

'The psychologist told me stuff I could do to make it better.'

'They were giving me stuff to do and I was getting to work on it.'

'If I was in that situation again I would know what to do straight away.'

● Recommendation to a friend: when asked if they would now recommend the psychological service to a friend whom they knew had a similar problem to the one that they experienced, all the young people replied affirmatively.

'It helped me a lot so I know they [my friend] would be better for this.'

'Yes because then they can go and get the help they need.'

'I would ask my friend if he wanted to see one [a psychologist].'

Issues surrounding other ways of accessing the psychological aervice

● Walk-in service: one participant thought that a self-referring walk-in service, located in the school, would be a useful development. Several of the other participants agreed.

'If you have got something wrong with you, you can go and talk to them.'

'It would be your decision whether you want to see them or not.'

'You can just go along.'

Results: Part 2 – compliance with PIs

Table 2 describes Renfrewshire Psychological Service's compliance with the previously mentioned PIs that are currently used to assess the quality of service provided to children and young people.

Discussion

Analysis of responses from the focus group suggests that for those young people involved, Renfrewshire Psychological Service complies with the PIs used to assess the quality of service provided for children and young people. There is one exception, however, and that is the lack of availability of printed leaflets about the service specifically written for young people.

The responses of the participants in this focus group indicate that the service is highly valued by the young people who use it. However, some concerns were expressed about the referral process, and in particular, some of the young people reported that they were unaware a referral had been made until either their parents or a member of the teaching staff told them an appointment with a psychologist had been arranged for them. In addition, not all the young people were aware they could exercise choice regarding contact with an educational psychologist (EP). They were generally satisfied, though, with issues concerning confidentiality and privacy.

The young people spoke very favourably about their relationship with the psychologist. In particular, the focus group participants emphasised that they felt their psychologist listened to them in detail, respected them and their opinions and took them seriously. They also commented on the importance of the psychologist giving them practical advice to use in future difficult situations. Great significance is attached to written reports. The young people regard these as important both for themselves and for others. However, they noted that reports need to be presented in an accessible style for young people. The focus group also observed that children and young people should have the automatic right to see reports about themselves from around the age of eight years or so.

It is clear from the results that contact with the psychological service does have a positive impact on its users. The young people felt their lives had been enhanced by this service, and they particularly valued psychological advice and strategies that enabled them to take control over their own lives. All the young people consulted did say they would recommend the service to a friend who had a similar problem to the one they experienced.

Two suggested developments to the psychological service were identified by the participants of the focus group:

1. Any written report should be discussed with the young person before being distributed, and the young person should always receive a personal copy of that report.

2. The service should establish a self-referral walk-in facility in each school, enabling young people from the age of 13 years to seek psychological advice independently.

The focus group results will be used by the psychological service to inform EPs about perceived strengths and weaknesses, and to suggest possible changes in the way the service operates. In this way, the focus group findings will inform the on-going process of service development.

Use of a focus group in this study demonstrated that it is a feasible, practical and helpful way to engage young users of the psychological service in discussions about its value.

However, ethical standards need to be clarified and maintained throughout, and researchers have to ensure that participants make a fully informed and free choice to become involved. Difficulties in running the group emerged, such as ensuring each young person had ample opportunity to speak, facilitating discussions between young people rather than directed through the moderators, keeping the discussion relevant to the key questions in the focus group within flexible parameters, and generating an accepting atmosphere in which the young people felt at ease with the moderators and each other. All of these potential difficulties, however, can be resolved with planning and sensitive management.

Conclusions

The focus group methodology provides a useful strategy for engaging young users of the psychological service in discussions about its effectiveness and offers a useful platform for consulting with children and young people.

Address for correspondence

Dr Richard C. Woolfson, Depute Principal Psychologist, Carbrook Street, Paisley PA1 2NW, UK.
E-mail: richard.woolfson@ntlworld.com

Volumes 22, 23 and 24 (2005–07): Shortlisted papers

Integrated children's services – implications for the profession
by Roger Booker, vol 22(4), 127–142.

Developing a community psychology orientation in an educational psychology service
by Phil Stringer, Julia Powell and Sheila Burton, vol 23(1), 59–67.

Educational psychology: The fall and rise of therapy
by Tommy MacKay, vol 24(1), 7–18.

A framework for the delivery of cognitive behaviour therapy in the educational psychology context
by Anne Greig, vol 24(1), 19–35.

Panel Members
Convenor: Theresa Bolton, educational psychologist, East Sussex
Alison Farmer, acting principal educational psychologist, Camden
Peter Farrell, professor of educational psychology, University of Manchester

Introduction by the panel

Of the articles that we considered, we have chosen Tommy MacKay's paper on *The fall and rise of therapy* within educational psychology. Why did we select this article? To start with, it provides an eloquent and reflective account of the profession's journey towards extending its range of services for schools, children and families. The paper is timely as it concerns the emotional well-being and mental health of young people and questions who are the most appropriate professionals to offer therapy, thereby feeding into active debates within educational psychology services. The place for therapy within the plethora of services offered by 21st century EPs will need to be justified and promoted, if it is to continue its recent upward trend.

MacKay presents a coherent description of the effect of changing legislative and cultural influences on educational psychologists' practice over time, drawing attention to key issues and tensions. It charts our faltering affections with therapy, taking an historical lens to how we have arrived at our present position, one that hints at more to come. At a time of new training routes into the profession, and increasing re-organisation of services into integrated multi-professional teams, MacKay's paper is welcome and thought provoking. What is the role for therapy in our evolving professional identity?

Today's schools seek to promote well-being and health, including mental health. It is, therefore, important for EPs to have the confidence and skills necessary to support schools in this challenging and demanding area. To suggest that these skills should be the preserve of fellow psychologists within child and adolescent mental health services (CAMHS) is to potentially create artificial divides between the psychologies, to the possible detriment of children and young people. MacKay challenges us to consider the appropriateness of the different psychologies offering discrete approaches to supporting the mental health of the nation's future workforce. Indeed, the traditional settings of clinics for therapy are not always the most pragmatic, or helpful for all clients.

If the Government's commitment to a programme of improved access to psychological therapies is taken as an intention to address mental health needs as a mainstream issue, then raising awareness of the potential for EPs to contribute to this programme is important not only for the profession but also for those with whom we work. The mental health and emotional well-being of the parents, children and young people who make up an EP's client group has long been of primary concern, given the strong link between these factors and the development of self-regulated behaviour, effective peer relationships, and academic attainment.

Educational psychologists are well practised in providing a bridge between universal and specialist services, whether through consultation and/or direct intervention. MacKay makes a well argued case for EPs to rise to the challenge of reconstruction and in so doing to re-visit, and re-apply ourselves to the practice of direct therapeutic work to support positive outcomes for vulnerable young people.

Educational psychologists as a 'therapeutic resource' continue to challenge both management and practice on the ground. MacKay offers a pertinent and timely overview for our profession's consideration, and as such is a welcome contribution to this special edition of the publication.

Theresa Bolton, Alison Farmer,
Peter Farrell

Address for correspondence
Theresa Bolton, Hilltop House, Buckland Hill, Cousley Wood, Wadhurst, East Sussex, TN5 6QT.
E-mail: theresab@gotadsl.co.uk

Educational psychology: The fall and rise of therapy

Tommy MacKay

Abstract

This paper considers the historical place of therapy in the early development of educational psychology. It then discusses reasons for its decline in terms of the reconstruction of the profession, increasingly demarcated professional boundaries, a predominant focus on education and the impact of special educational needs legislation on professional practice. It argues, however, that it is time for therapy to be rehabilitated in educational psychology, proposing this as a historical inevitability that is now supported by the rising profile of mental health issues in children and young people, the new evidence base for therapy and changing perspectives on the nature of applied psychology. It concludes by outlining the signs of a rising commitment to therapy within the profession and asserts the role of educational psychologists as a key therapeutic resource for children and young people.

I N EDUCATIONAL PSYCHOLOGY the term "therapy" is seldom heard.' Thus Indoe (1995) sought to rehabilitate the concept of therapy into an arena that had in large measure abandoned it – the arena of educational psychology in the mid-1990s. It was the latter days of a period in which such abandonment would hold centre stage in that arena – a period marked by a number of mantras, such as 'educational psychology is not a therapeutic service'. It was a period indeed in which not only therapeutic work but any direct work with the individual child or young person was almost viewed in some quarters as being undesirable or, at best, second rate. That such mantras might be historically, psychologically and conceptually bankrupt did not seem to be considered, and so for a time the question of their legitimacy or validity was largely unchallenged. Thus the expert skills in direct individual work of a profession founded on the study and application of individual psychology were devalued and marginalised.

It was not that individual work, including therapeutic work, had ceased to exist (Hayes, 1996; MacKay & Vassie, 1998), or that the supporters of individual therapy questioned the necessity and value of systemic interventions in schools, albeit recog-

nising the relative lack of a robust evidence base to validate such interventions. Nor indeed did the new mantras pass completely unchallenged. For example, MacKay (1990), in a paper entitled 'Individuals or systems: Have educational psychologists sold their birthright?', feared that 'a whole generation of psychologists may become deskilled in the methods of individual assessment and the techniques of therapeutic intervention'. He argued that the pioneers of the profession were individual psychologists, systems psychologists and academic psychologists, and that this threefold foundation represented the inalienable birthright of professional educational psychology. The importance of direct individual work in relation to mental health was also the focus of a DECP Working Party from 1993 to 1995 on reappraising the role of educational psychologists in working with child and adolescent psychological and mental health needs (Indoe *et al.*, 1996).

Historical foundations of therapy in educational psychology

The formal development of educational psychology as an applied discipline in the UK had its origins in the early decades of the twentieth century. In 1913 Cyril Burt became the first educational psychologist in the UK on his appointment to London County Council, and his contribution shaped the structure for professional practice for the next half century, especially in relation to assessment and intervention for individual children. Parallel events took place in Scotland, where in 1923 the first post of a child psychologist was established when Kennedy Fraser was appointed by Glasgow Education Committee as a psychological adviser. Later in the same decade educational psychology clinics were set up at the Universities of Glasgow and of Edinburgh (McKnight, 1978).

The context in which these developments in educational settings took place was governed by the parent discipline of child psychology, which had become an established subject in the universities by the end of the 19th century. In 1884 Francis Galton had opened in London his anthropometric laboratory for the study of individual differences, and had advocated the scientific study of children. A psychological laboratory was opened in 1896 by James Sully, a founder member of the British Psychological Society and convener of its first meeting in 1901. In his classic *Studies of childhood* (Sully, 1896) he outlined the importance of 'the careful, methodic study of the individual child', and teachers and parents were invited to take difficult children to his laboratory for examination and advice on treatment. Sully paved the way for a new kind of specialist to work with children in the educational sphere.

Two quite different but very major influences shaped the way in which educational psychology would develop and their impact is still apparent in the emphases of services today. The first was the mental testing movement, with its focus on the assessment of individual differences in children. The second was the child guidance movement, with its focus on treatment of children with emotional and behavioural difficulties. It was the latter influence that led to the early emphasis on psychological therapies designed to support children and young people who were experiencing difficulties in their emotional and behavioural adjustment.

The way in which the joint influence of mental testing and child guidance shaped service development was somewhat different in England and Wales and in Scotland. In England and Wales a school psychological service was funded through education services, while educational psychologists also worked in child guidance clinics as members of a medically directed team of psychiatrist, social worker and psychologist. Scottish child guidance clinics, also frequently operating on a multidisciplinary basis, were directed by educational psychologists and were funded by education.

In Scotland, education authorities were empowered from 1946 to establish their child guidance clinics on a broad statutory foundation (MacKay, 1996). This became mandatory on all authorities in 1969 and it continues to govern Scottish education authority psychological services today. The remit related to children, and later young people until they reached age 19, who were described in the statutes as 'handicapped, backward and difficult' (since 2004 as having 'additional support needs'). The official guidance supporting the statutes made it clear that this covered a very wide range of educational, developmental and other difficulties, including those who suffered from 'emotional instability or psychological disturbance'. Thus a broad foundation was established not only for work of an educational nature but also for therapeutic interventions in relation to children's mental health.

It was against this background of early developments in relation to children with mental health difficulties that the routine therapeutic involvement of educational psychologists developed. In some services, the records kept for annual statistics were divided between 'educational' and 'clinical' cases and it was these latter cases, covering all forms of difficulties in development and adjustment, that were the recipients of therapeutic interventions.

Tommy MacKay

The fall of therapy

There were several reasons for the changes by which educational psychologists over a period of time largely ceased to identify themselves as psychological therapists. Four are outlined here: the reconstruction of educational psychology, increasingly demarcated professional boundaries, the focus on education and the impact of legislation.

The reconstruction of educational psychology
The reconstruction of the profession through the 1980s was an essential process in the transformation of educational psychology into a robust, highly accountable and evidence-based profession. Undoubtedly the main catalyst was the work of Gillham and his colleagues with the publication of *Reconstructing educational psychology* (Gillham, 1978). The concept of professional 'reconstruction' paralleled developments in other disciplines from the beginning of the 1970s onwards. Shulman (1970) was reconstructing educational research, followed by Armistead (1974) who was reconstructing social psychology.

The essential element of reconstruction was a move away from the psychologist as individual caseworker to being an agent for systemic change in schools and other systems, using models drawn from organisational psychology and other disciplines. The arguments for change were compelling and were eloquently expressed and exemplified. A robust critique was offered of reactive, individual methods of working in terms of efficiency, efficacy and equity. For the next 20 years and more the educational psychology literature was to be dominated by the agenda for change (Acklaw, 1990; Jensen *et al.*, 2002; Stobie, 2002a, 2002b).

Change driven by arguments based on efficiency and efficacy was for all practical purposes unanswerable. There could be no justification for an accountable profession to work at individual level with a tiny proportion of the population requiring its services. What could be the possible impact of any profession that was concerned with the individual alone? The entire system was marked by a large number of children and young people who had significant problems in their learning, behaviour and development. However, the number in question far exceeded anything within the reasonable compass of individual assessment and intervention. The application of the knowledge base of educational psychology at systemic level was crucial. Although it was apparent in the systemic work of pioneers like Burt, whose contribution influenced entire systems right to the level of national policy formulation by government committees (Hearnshaw, 1979), it was not a feature of the work of educational psychology services immediately prior to the reconstruction movement.

In terms of equity of service provision, the model of offering individual assessment and treatment was also open to challenge. It was not just that some received a service while others did not, but that questions could be raised as to who were the recipients of the services offered. Many years ago it was shown that while the mental health issues and other problems with which the caring professions are concerned are overrepresented in the lower socio-economic groups, these groups are often underrepresented in the distribution of resources and in the extent to which they can gain access to them (Hollingshead & Redlich, 1958). Tudor Hart (1971) described this as the 'inverse care law', whereby resources are distributed in inverse proportion to need. More recently this has been demonstrated in an educational context (MacKay, 2000c; Sacker *et al.*, 2001).

One of the many advantages of reconstruction was that it presented an opportunity for the profession to stand back and challenge every dogma by which it had ever been guided. While this process was not without its risks and indeed its mistakes, it was crucial to professional renewal and regeneration. Thus, the entire foundation of practice was challenged, and the old models were weighed in the balance and found wanting. Significantly, it was recognised that applied psychology in general, and educational psychology in particular, was still operating on a 'medical model'. Assessment and intervention were governed by a medical analogy based on 'within-child' deficits. The whole language and structure of the profession echoed the model in its practice, its remit and its vocabulary. Educational psychologists offered 'treatment' to children with impairments and disabilities in settings that were often described as (and in an interesting anachronism of Scottish legislation are still defined as including) 'clinics'.

The rejection of the medical model resulted in a 'paradigm shift' (Kirkaldy, 1997) towards what was essentially a psychological or even educational model in which the psychologist became a consultative colleague working alongside parents, teachers and other key adults with primary responsibility for assessment and intervention in the child's normal context. The new perspective was interactionist and ecological, with the educational psychologist as a collaborative colleague working with others for effective change in the social ecology of children and young people. The emphasis was fundamentally different from the model of the psychologist as an expert providing therapy to remedy the problems of the individual.

Increasingly demarcated professional boundaries
The increasing demarcation of professional boundaries was a historically inevitable process in the development of applied psychology from being a largely generic professional discipline to a highly specialised one. It is a process that has been incisively delineated by Bender (1976) in his seminal work on community psychology. First there are the 'pioneers', those who break new ground, forming a profession in its embryonic stages and demonstrating its utility to society. Next come the 'consolidators', those who generally do not match the exceptional work of the pioneers, but who establish the profession by setting up training courses and a careers structure, by defining and restricting the role and by making the profession a monopoly.

This is precisely the process that has

taken place in applied psychology. Those of us who have worked in the field for a lengthy period of time remember days in which distinctions between 'educational' and 'clinical' child psychology were largely an artefact of employment arrangements, and when psychologists moved easily between these (and other) psychological specialisms by a process that later came to be called 'lateral transfer' – that is, an applied psychologist moved between one specialist description and another according to the employment context that obtained at the time. With the passage of time these arrangements became increasingly demarcated, but the process has been of such recent origin that most of the 'divisions' within professional psychology have only in the past few years moved out of 'grandparenting' arrangements into highly formalised qualifications and entry requirements.

This is not to say that the process of specialisation and formal qualifications lacks validity and utility. The development of new arrangements has reflected a vastly increased knowledge base where higher levels of study, skill and expertise are a fundamental requirement for practice at a satisfactory level. It is impossible as the academic evidence base advances to maintain a position of being a 'generic' psychologist without extensive study of a number of specialist areas. This is the rationale that underlies the current demarcation within the British Psychological Society, with many 'Divisions' each of which has its own qualifications and entry requirements – educational, clinical, forensic, occupational, clinical neuropsychological, counselling and sports and exercise psychology, with further routes for 'teaching' and 'research' in psychology. The potential for yet further subdivision is considerable, the next obvious 'Division' perhaps being 'traffic and transport psychology'.

However, while these divisions of the subject matter of the core discipline have rightly reflected a developing and distinctive evidence base, one outcome has been to imply limitations to previously established professional practice. The case of 'therapy' is an obvious one. What are educational psychologists doing with 'clinical' cases? Is therapy for mental health issues an 'educational' concern? Furthermore, is there not now a Division of Counselling Psychology, and also a register of 'psychologists specialising in psychotherapy', so are educational psychologists acting with propriety if they view their core functions as falling within these domains?

This is a fundamental dilemma for applied psychology, not only in how its various domains relate within psychology itself, but also in the interrelationships it has with other disciplines. Are assessment and intervention in speech and language difficulties less of a psychological specialism because of the expansion of the old established therapeutic discipline of 'speech therapy' into the wider language and communication arena? Will psychologists eventually opt out of the field of sensory assessment and intervention – the absolute heartland of psychology – because the discipline of occupational therapy has found new ground there?

Clearly psychology must retain its foundations in all of these areas. Equally, each discipline within psychology is not expected to cease operations in its old established territory because of the development of new specialisms. The British Psychological Society has appropriately dealt with this issue by stressing that professional applications of psychology are based on 'competence' and not on the specific nature of the activity being carried out. Can we really imagine a vibrant and competent educational psychology profession demarcating its activities to avoid the work that arises in clinical psychology, health psychology, clinical neuropsychology and other fields? Examples of the invalidity of such an approach are developed in MacKay (2005) in considering the relationship between educational psychology and clinical neuropsychology.

Nevertheless, the impact of increased demarcation and specialisation remains, and it has had its influence on educational psychol-

ogy. 'Clinical' work is increasingly viewed as the domain of the clinical psychologist, while 'therapy' sounds like a specialist term that only certain people are qualified to carry out. These may be some other species of psychologist, such as a 'counselling psychologist', or someone who is not a psychologist at all, but who has done a one-year course to become some description of 'therapist'. Meanwhile the whole field of therapy itself has become more formalised and regulated, with many different therapeutic applications now having their own pathways to accreditation.

The combination of factors becomes self-fulfilling. Educational psychologists find themselves with ever decreasing resources to provide therapeutic services. As a result, they spend ever decreasing time engaged in therapy. Therefore, their competence in therapeutic interventions becomes less and less. The old skills wither, confidence declines and it becomes increasingly obvious that we are not, and indeed could no longer reasonably claim to be, a 'therapeutic service'.

The focus on education

It is proposed here that over a period of time educational psychology has undergone a systematic transformation from being a broad 'child psychology' specialism into being a narrow 'educational' specialism. Unlike some parts of the world where 'educational psychology' has had no real existence as a discipline but only 'school psychology', the traditions of educational psychology in the UK, as outlined above, are rooted in the broad application of child psychology both in schools and in other settings. Increasingly, however, the profession has become defined as a 'school psychological service', and even within the strictures of that definition the emphasis has been very much on a narrow understanding of education in curricular terms rather than a wider interest that incorporates mental health.

A principal reason for this narrower educational emphasis was the increasing rigidity of departmental boundaries through the

1980s and 1990s. The well-being of children and young people is addressed within public services through a variety of departments of which the most significant are health, education and social services. Through a long period in which successive governments were speaking about 'joined up working' in these services the actual arrangements by which they were funded and administered was becoming more rigid and inflexible. Examples continued to abound of meetings and reviews involving professionals working with young people from a variety of disciplines, but real professional collaborations on a multidisciplinary basis were not in abundance (MacKay, 2006). Meanwhile, collaborative enterprises for addressing the mental health needs of children and young people, such as the child guidance clinics, were being disbanded or cut back throughout the country (Mittler, 1990), and educational psychology links with those that remained were becoming 'residual' (Day & Fleming, 1996).

In addition there was – and continues to be – a major political imperative for schools to increase their focus on promoting basic educational competence in the core subjects of the curriculum. Basic literacy became the key emphasis, with a level of governmental prescription and inspection that was unprecedented. This emphasis extended across every age range. From the nursery through to school leaving age the pressure mounted on educational establishments to produce measurable results. The new focus was on audits, targets, standards and statistics.

Certainly, there was no denying the crucial importance of attaining these core competences and of placing them at the heart of the educational curriculum. Also, the basic issues surrounding literacy and the wider aspects of learning were key territory for the educational psychologist to make an effective contribution at the level both of the system and of the individual child. Nevertheless, educational psychologists as accountable professionals supporting the key objectives of the education system were increasingly expected to have a central focus on these curricular areas, and on supporting pupils who were experiencing difficulties in school learning. In a pressurised and competitive world of league tables, the educational environment was hardly one in which therapeutic needs were going to be at the forefront.

The impact of legislation

From the beginning of the 1980s educational legislation for children and young people with additional support needs vastly increased both in extent and in complexity. This gave educational psychologists in England and Wales their one statutory duty in relation to the Statement of Needs, and it laid additional statutory requirements on Scottish psychologists in relation to the Record of Needs (discontinued since 2004). The impact of this legislation on the profession of educational psychology is widely documented (Boxer *et al.*, 1998; Farrell *et al.*, 2006; MacKay, 2000b; Woods, 1994). In summary, it depleted the profession's resources and it narrowed and distorted the contribution that psychologists might have made.

As to depletion of resources, the servicing of the requirements of the legislation was time consuming, not only in carrying out large numbers of statutory assessments but also in dealing with any appeals. Bennett (1998) reported that a tribunal hearing involved an average of around 10 hours in prior preparation alone, with over 20 per cent of psychologists spending more than 20 hours. Boxer *et al.* (1998) expressed concerns that an increasing workload and short time scales threatened the quality and impact of the work undertaken. In Scotland, services indicated that this area of work was consuming such a disproportionate amount of time that resources had to be deflected from other functions (MacKay, 2003). Surveys of practice indicated that educational psychologists were spending an average of 15 hours collating reports and writing the draft Record of Needs for each recorded child (Thomson *et al.*, 1995).

As to narrowing and distorting the contribution made by psychologists, the balance of work shifted inexorably towards statutory assessment and report writing at the expense of other areas (Boxer *et al.*, 1998), and innovative practice was frequently squeezed out (Thomson, 1996). Woods (1994) warned of the dangers to the future of the profession in having priorities distorted towards the demands of the legislation, and pictured 'a world without statementing' in which psychologists used the skills and evidence base of psychology itself to deliver a wide range of effective services.

It is hardly surprising that in a profession where one activity – carrying out work related to statutory assessment – gained such excessive prominence, the focus was turned away from other areas of potentially fruitful and effective psychological interventions. It was not a context in which therapy stood any reasonable chance of being seen as a priority in terms of allocation of resources. MacKay (2002) saw educational psychologists 'caught up in the Statement of Needs, while their old, established clinical and therapeutic skills atrophy'.

The rise of therapy

Indoe's (1995) remark that the term 'therapy' is seldom heard in educational psychology continued to be applicable to the profession through the remaining years of the 20th century. More recently, however, the context has begun to change and the place of therapy has been revisited. Just as there were clear reasons for its fall, so there are clear reasons for its rise. These may be summarised under the headings of: a historically inevitable process, the rise in mental health problems in childhood, the establishment of an evidence base for psychological therapies and a re-examination of roles and boundaries in applied psychology.

First, the historical inevitability of something so central and so long established as therapy rising again is part of a recurrent process in professional reconstruction. Structures and roles are first established in a new profession and for a period they remain

essentially unchallenged. Then the process of reconstruction begins, and the old ways are questioned, found to be flawed and therefore rejected. Sweeping reform establishes new structures and roles, also untested and unchallenged. Then in due course, a fresh perspective leads to some of the old ways being re-examined. Their enduring value is recognised and they become rehabilitated but on a more robust footing than they were previously. This necessity of 'diversion from diversion' (Rappaport & Stewart, 1997) is paradigmatic and is not unique to reconstruction in educational psychology.

It is proposed that in relation to therapy the time for it to re-establish its place in educational psychology practice has come. The new paradigms that have emphasised systemic and strategic roles in schools are now embedded in routine practice. Their value is recognised not only within the profession but also by service users. For example, there is evidence that in the last 10 years the perceived value of the contribution of educational psychologists to schools has increased significantly, and that a central, strategic role in schools is the single best predictor of the perceived value of the contribution made (Boyle & MacKay, in press).

The same study, however, provided strong evidence that schools continue to view individual casework as being of crucial importance in the role of the educational psychologist. The review of educational psychology in England and Wales also reported that most respondent groups highly valued their contact with psychologists, but 'would have welcomed more, particularly in the area of therapy and intervention' (Farrell *et al.*, 2006). Service users are ready to receive therapeutic services, and the profession is well placed to provide them.

Second, the rise in the prevalence of mental health problems in children and young people over a considerable period of time is well documented (Rutter & Smith, 1995). It includes depression, suicide rates, anorexia nervosa and other serious eating disorders, alcohol problems, drug abuse and emotional and behavioural difficulties in general, with the evidence pointing to a continuing rise in these difficulties. Epidemiological studies suggest overall population prevalence rates for child and adolescent mental health disorders ranging upwards from a minimum of 12 per cent (Davis *et al.* 2000). Meltzer *et al.* (2000) in their survey of the mental health of children and adolescents in Great Britain reported that 20 per cent may be described as having a mental health problem.

These disorders lead to high levels of personal distress for the young people and families involved and they show continuity into adulthood (Robins & Rutter, 1990; Rutter *et al.*, 2006). However, only a small proportion of these children and young people receive any form of specialist help. Estimates of the numbers with disorders who do receive help have ranged from 10 per cent to 21 per cent (Davis *et al.*, 2000). Reasons for this include the inaccessibility or unavailability of appropriate services and the perceived stigma of attendance at specialist health services. It is recognised that resources are inadequate and that it is 'impractical to expect current specialist child and adolescent mental health services to cope with significantly increased demand' (Davis *et al.*, 2000).

It is clear in any event that mental health issues on this scale are not going to be tackled on a reactive basis through individual interventions either by psychologists or by other specialist professionals, and that systemic and preventative initiatives are required (Albee & Gullotta, 1997). The case for prevention and for tackling the system at the macro-level rather than the individual at the micro-level has been convincingly argued by Prilleltensky and Nelson (2000) in their critical agenda for priorities in promoting child and family wellness. Their view is that specialist services spend almost all their resources fire fighting, and they point to the futility of continuing to 'focus on counselling, therapy or person-centred prevention as the main vehicles for the promotion of wellness'.

The need for prevention, however, does not detract from the need for therapeutic services. No matter how important the role of fire prevention, we still must have people to put out the fires. There will always be a need for expert individual work in the field of child mental health. It must also be recognised that not all needs can be addressed by a focus on the child's social ecology. There are also 'within-child' variables – disorders, impairments, disabilities – that need to be identified, assessed and treated (MacKay, 2000a).

Addressing the mental health issues of children and young people has become a central political imperative to which public agencies in health, education and social services are expected to respond. This emphasis on mental health, together with an increased focus on integrated children's services, with agencies across health, education and social services working in collaboration, provides a key opportunity for educational psychologists to make a significant contribution to this area and to include therapy in the range of services they routinely offer.

Third, a robust evidence base has now been established for psychological therapies (see Greig in this issue). At a former time when therapeutic work was very much more prevalent in educational psychology services the evidence base for its efficacy was scant. Now, when there is an established evidence base, therapeutic work is relatively scant. Earlier approaches to examining the efficacy of therapy were generally inadequate. With the exception of a large body of evidence for behaviour therapy to address highly focused problems, approaches to assessing evidence did not sufficiently differentiate between different therapeutic approaches or different disorders. Also, the terms 'therapy' and 'psychotherapy' were usually associated with psychodynamic approaches. These tended to be long-term therapies that either had no discernible outcomes or that did not readily lend themselves to outcome appraisal (see, for example, Eysenck, 1952).

In recent years therapy has become much more focused in terms both of its methodology and of the particular difficulties it addresses. This has facilitated the development of a very substantial evidence base covering many areas, such as cognitive behaviour therapy for mood disorders and EMDR (eye movement desensitisation and reprocessing) for post-traumatic stress disorder. Educational psychology in seeking to be an evidence-based profession can therefore appropriately embrace therapeutic interventions and apply them where they have known effectiveness.

Finally, it is clear that roles and boundaries within applied psychology are being re-examined. It is not sustainable for a discipline that has such a common foundation in its knowledge base and methods to continue with ever increasing levels of demarcation, supported by very long and completely separate training routes. Alternatives are now being proposed in comprehensive terms. For example, Kinderman (2005) has called for an 'applied psychology revolution' with a single three-year doctoral training, with specialisation into the current branches of applied psychology in the third year.

The reviews of educational psychology services both in Scotland and in England and Wales have recognised the need for more shared practice, cooperative working and integration across the disciplines of applied psychology. The Scottish review (Scottish Executive, 2002) recommended that steps should be taken towards educational and clinical child psychology services developing more integrated training and working arrangements. The English review went so far as to recommend that 'professional organisations representing EPs should begin discussions about the possible eventual merger of the two professions, child clinical and educational psychologists' (Farrell *et al.*, 2006, p.12). Viewing therapy and mental health issues as the province of another branch of psychology will not be helpful as applied psychology moves towards more integrated approaches.

Therapy rehabilitated: Evidence from the profession

There is evidence from the profession that therapy is being rehabilitated within educational psychology, and that new trends may reverse the force of Indoe's earlier observation that the term is seldom heard. This is reflected in official reports, in data gathered from the field and in a number of wider developments within the profession.

In terms of official reports, a significant change may be discerned in the six years that elapsed between the Working Group report on educational psychology services in England (Department for Education and Employment, 2000; Kelly & Gray, 2000) and the recent review of the functions and contribution of educational psychologists in England and Wales (Farrell et al., 2006). The Working Group report contains no reference to therapy, although it does refer to counselling services to support children's emotional development. The new review report contains a large number of direct references to therapy, including a recommendation that with the trend towards reduction of statutory work educational psychologists should expand into areas 'where their skills and knowledge can be used to greater effect, e.g. in group and individual therapy' (Farrell et al., 2006, p.106).

The Scottish review also pointed to the rehabilitation of therapy and its place in holistic psychological interventions across home, school and community. In addition, it provided the strongest confirmation from the field of the readiness of the profession to expand its therapeutic work. About 60 per cent of Scotland's educational psychologists responded to a survey regarding core psychological activities that had been compromised by the pressures of non-psychological work. Of these, 155 respondents provided specific and unprompted examples of work they believed required more prominence. The most recurrent theme, raised by over 100 respondents, related to therapeutic interventions with children and families.

In terms of wider developments in the profession there are many signs of a revived interest in therapy and mental health issues. This has been reflected in recent literature locating these issues firmly within the context of educational psychology practice (for example, Greig, 2004a, 2004b; Greig & MacKay, 2005; and this current issue devoted to therapeutic interventions). Educational psychologists have been very much to the fore in the practice of specific therapies such as EMDR and solution-focused brief therapy, and in a few cases full accreditation in areas such as cognitive and behavioural psychotherapy has been attained.

Conclusions

This paper has argued for the rehabilitation of therapy in educational psychology practice. It has outlined the reasons why therapeutic interventions declined from their former prominence within the profession, but it has also examined the basis on which these skills and approaches are again required. Reference has been made to the high prevalence of mental health issues in children and young people, to the value placed on therapeutic work by service users and to the fact that the profession has identified therapy as an area that should be expanded.

It has been estimated that in a secondary school of 1,000 pupils, around 50 will be seriously depressed and 100 will be suffering significant distress (Young Minds, 2000). Where educational psychologists have responded to these contexts by providing carefully targeted therapeutic services where they are most needed (such as the services provided by the editors of this issue in Argyll and Bute), these services have not only been effective but in many cases have been of crucial significance to individual children and young people. In some cases, such as mood disorders in Asperger's syndrome, they have

made the key differences that have made mainstream placements sustainable; in others, such as obsessive-compulsive disorder, they have been the essential ingredient in enabling children to attend school at all and improving their future life prospects; in others, such as depression and attempted suicide, they may have been the difference between life and death.

Educational psychologists are a key therapeutic resource for young people, especially in educational contexts such as schools. They are the professionals most thoroughly embedded in educational systems; they have the widest training in child and adolescent psychology and are therefore best poised to be generic child psychologists (MacKay, 2006); and, despite lack of resources, they are in fact the most plentiful group of child psychologists employed in public services. If mental health issues in educational settings are not addressed by educational psychologists through a fresh commitment to therapeutic work then they will be bought in from other sources.

The effective development of therapeutic services has implications for postgraduate training courses, for continuing professional development and for service organisation. Such services, in combination with a wide range of other psychological initiatives including preventative and systemic interventions, could represent a key contribution to evidence-based educational psychology practice.

Note: The author is an educational psychologist and an accredited cognitive behavioural psychotherapist.

Address for correspondence

Dr Tommy MacKay, Psychology Consultancy Services, Ardoch House, Cardross, Dumbartonshire G82 5EW.
E-mail: Tommy@ardoch.fsnet.co.uk

References

Acklaw, J. (1990). Change and the management of educational psychology services in England and Wales. *School Psychology International, 11*, 3–7.

Albee, G. & Gullotta, T. (Eds.) (1997). *Primary prevention works.* London: Sage.

Armistead, N. (Ed.) (1974). *Reconstructing social psychology.* Oxford: Penguin.

Bender, M. (1976). *Community psychology.* London: Methuen.

Bennett, P. (1998). Special educational needs tribunals. *Educational Psychology in Practice, 14*(3), 203–208.

Boxer, R., Foot, R., Greaves, K. & Harris, J. (1998). LEA criteria and the nature of EP assessment. *Educational Psychology in Practice, 14*(2), 128–134.

Boyle, J. & MacKay, T. (in press). Evidence for the efficacy of systemic models of practice from a cross-sectional survey of schools' satisfaction with their educational psychologists. *Educational Psychology in Practice.*

Davis, H., Day, C., Cox, A. & Cutler, L. (2000). Child and adolescent mental health needs: Assessment and service implications in an inner city area. *Clinical Child Psychology and Psychiatry, 5*(2), 169–188.

Day, S. & Fleming, L. (1996). Findings from studies into EPs and child guidance and EPS auditing of EBD work. *Educational and Child Psychology, 13*(1), 23–31.

Department for Education and Employment (2000). *Educational psychology services (England): Current role, good practice and future directions. Report of the Working Group.* Nottingham: Department for Education and Employment.

Eysenck, H. (1952). The effects of psychotherapy: An evaluation. *Journal of Consulting Psychology, 16*, 319–324.

Farrell, P., Woods, K., Lewis, S., Rooney, S., Squires, G. & O'Connor, M. (2006). *A review of the functions and contribution of educational psychologists in England and Wales in the light of Every child matters: Change for children.* Nottingham: Department for Education and Employment.

Gillham, B. (Ed.) (1978). *Reconstructing educational psychology.* London: Croom Helm.

Greig, A. (2004a). Childhood depression – Part I: Does it need to be dealt with only by health professionals? *Educational and Child Psychology, 21*(4), 43–54.

Greig, A. (2004b). Childhood depression – Part II: The role of the educational psychologist in the recognition and intervention of childhood depression. *Educational and Child Psychology, 21*(4), 55–66.

Greig, A. & MacKay, T. (2005). Asperger's syndrome and cognitive behaviour therapy: New applications for educational psychologists.

Educational and Child Psychology, 22(4), 4–15.

Hayes, S. (1996). 'Teasing out' more qualitative aspects from the Working Party questionnaire data source. *Educational and Child Psychology, 13*(1), 13–22.

Hearnshaw, L. (1979). *Cyril Burt: Psychologist.* London: Hodder & Stoughton.

Hollingshead, A. & Redlich, F. (1958). *Social class and mental illness.* New York: Wiley.

Indoe, D. (1995). Therapeutic interventions: Editorial. *Educational and Child Psychology, 12*(4), 4.

Indoe, D., Lunt, I. & Wolfendale, S. (Eds.) (1996). *Educational psychologists, mental health and adolescent behaviour.* Special issue, *Educational and Child Psychology, 13*(1).

Jensen, A., Malcolm, L., Phelps, F. & Stoker, R. (2002). Changing patterns of thinking: Individuals and organisations. *Educational Psychology in Practice, 18*(1), 35–45.

Kelly, D. & Gray, C. (2000). *Educational psychology services (England): Current role, good practice and future directions. The research report.* Nottingham: Department for Education and Employment.

Kinderman, P. (2005). The applied psychology revolution. *The Psychologist, 18*, 744–746.

Kirkaldy, B. (1997). Contemporary tasks for psychological services in Scotland. *Educational Psychology in Scotland, 5*, 6–16.

MacKay, T. (1990). Individuals or systems: Have educational psychologists sold their birthright? *BPS Scottish Division of Educational and Child Psychology Newsletter, 1*, 1–9.

MacKay, T. (1996). The statutory foundations of Scottish educational psychology services. *Educational Psychology in Scotland, 3*, 3–9.

MacKay, T. (2000a). Commentary on Prilleltensky and Nelson, 'Promoting child and family wellness: priorities for psychological and social intervention'. *Journal of Community and Applied Social Psychology, 10*, 113–116.

MacKay, T. (2000b). Educational psychology and the future of special educational needs legislation. *Educational and Child Psychology, 17*(2), 27–35.

MacKay, T. (2000c). The Record of Needs: Does its distribution across Scotland reflect real need? *Education in the North, 7*, 29–34.

MacKay, T. (2002). The future of educational psychology. *Educational Psychology in Practice, 18*(3), 245–253.

MacKay, T. (2003). Psychological services and their impact. In T. Bryce & W. Humes (Eds.), *Scottish Education* (2nd edn, pp.842–852). Edinburgh: Edinburgh University Press.

MacKay, T. (2005). The relationship of educational psychology and clinical neuropsychology. *Educational and Child Psychology, 22*(2), 7–17.

MacKay, T. (2006). The educational psychologist as community psychologist: Holistic child psychology across home, school and community. *Educational and Child Psychology, 23*(1), 7–13.

MacKay, T. & Vassie, C. (1998). Is Scottish educational psychology changing? The results of a 16-year time-sampling of the work of psychologists. *Abstracts of annual conference for educational psychologists in Scotland, 1998.* BPS Scottish Division of Educational Psychology.

McKnight, R.K. (1978). The development of child guidance services. In W.B. Dockrell, W.R. Dunn & A. Milne (Eds.), *Special education in Scotland* (pp.97–109). Edinburgh: Scottish Council for Research in Education.

Meltzer, H., Gartward, R., Goodman, R. & Ford, T. (2000). *Mental health of children and adolescents in Great Britain.* London: The Stationery Office.

Mittler, P. (1990). Too difficult to address? *Times Educational Supplement,* No. 3843, p.26.

Prilleltensky, I. & Nelson, G. (2000). Promoting child and family wellness: Priorities for psychological and social intervention. *Journal of Community and Applied Social Psychology, 10*(2), 85–105.

Rappaport, J. & Stewart, E. (1997). A critical look at critical psychology: Elaborating the questions. In D. Fox & I. Prilleltensky (Eds.), *Critical psychology: An introduction* (pp.301–317). London: Sage.

Robins, L. & Rutter, M. (1990). *Straight and devious pathways from childhood to adulthood.* Cambridge: Cambridge University Press.

Rutter, M., Kim-Cohen, J. & Maughan, B. (2006). Continuities and discontinuities in psychopathology between childhood and adult life. *Journal of Child Psychology and Psychiatry, 47*(3/4), 276–295.

Rutter, M. & Smith, D. (Eds.) (1995). *Psychosocial disorders in young people: Time trends and their causes.* Chichester: Wiley.

Sacker, A., Schoon, I. & Bartley, M. (2001). Sources of bias in special needs provision in mainstream primary schools: Evidence from two British cohort studies. *European Journal of Special Needs Education, 16*(3), 259–276.

Scottish Executive (2002). *Review of provision of educational psychology services in Scotland* (The Currie Report). Edinburgh: Scottish Executive.

Shulman, L.S. (1970). Reconstruction of educational research. *Review of Educational Research, 40,* 371–393.

Stobie, I. (2002a). Processes of 'change' and 'continuity' in educational psychology: Part I. *Educational Psychology in Practice, 18*(3), 203–212.

Stobie, I. (2002b). Processes of 'change' and 'continuity' in educational psychology: Part II. *Educational Psychology in Practice, 18*(3), 213–237.

Sully, J. (1896). *Studies in childhood.* London: Longmans Green.

Thomson, G.O.B., Stewart, M.E. & Ward, K.M. (1995). *Criteria for opening a Record of Needs: Report to the Scottish Office Education Department.* Edinburgh: Edinburgh University Press.

Thomson, L. (1996). Searching for a niche: Future directions for educational psychologists. *Educational Psychology in Practice, 12*(2), 99–106.

Tudor Hart, J. (1971). The inverse care law. *Lancet, 1,* 7696, 405–412.

Woods, K. (1994). Towards national criteria for special educational needs: Some conceptual and practical considerations for educational psychologists. *Educational Psychology in Practice, 10*(2), 85–92.

Young Minds (2000). *Whose crisis?* www.youngminds.org.uk/whosecrisis. Web page accessed 26 October 2006.